PENGUIN BOOKS

Real Fast Puddings

Nigel Slater is one of Britain's most highly regarded food writers – his simple, down-to-earth cooking has won him a huge following. He is the author of a collection of bestselling books, including the classics *Real Fast Food* and *Real Cooking*. His books have been shortlisted numerous times for the André Simon, Glenfiddich and Julia Childs Awards, and in 1998 his book, *Nigel Slater's Real Food* won the Glenfiddich Award. His next book, *Appetite*, published in 2000, went on to win the André Simon Cookbook of the Year Award.

He won the Glenfiddich Trophy in 1995 and has twice won Cookery Writer of the Year (1995 and 1999). In 1996 he was named Media Personality of the Year at the Good Food Awards and was awarded Best Newspaper Cookery Journalist in 1999.

His memoir *Toast*, published in 2003, won six awards, including the Glenfiddich and André Simon Awards, and British Biography of the Year.

Nigel Slater is Food Correspondent of the *Observer* and has written a much-loved weekly column for them for over a decade now. He is a regular contributor to Sainsbury's *The Magazine*.

D0262893

Also by Nigel Slater:

Real Fast Food
Real Fast Puddings
The 30-Minute Cook
Real Good Food
Real Cooking
Nigel Slater's Real Food
Appetite
Thirst
Toast: the story of a boy's hunger
The Kitchen Diaries

NIGEL SLATER

Real Fast Puddings

Over 200 desserts, savouries and
sweet snacks in 30 minutes

PENGUIN BOOKS

PENGUIN BOOKS

Published by the Penguin Group
Penguin Books Ltd, 80 Strand, London WC2R 0RL, England
Penguin Group (USA) Inc., 375 Hudson Street, New York, New York 10014, USA
Penguin Group (Canada), 90 Eglinton Avenue East, Suite 700, Toronto, Ontario, Canada M4P 2Y3
(a division of Pearson Penguin Canada Inc.)
Penguin Ireland, 25 St Stephen's Green, Dublin 2, Ireland
(a division of Penguin Books Ltd)
Penguin Group (Australia), 250 Camberwell Road, Camberwell, Victoria 3124, Australia
(a division of Pearson Australia Group Pty Ltd)
Penguin Books India Pvt Ltd, 11 Community Centre, Panchsheel Park, New Delhi – 110 017, India
Penguin Group (NZ), 67 Apollo Drive, Mairangi Bay, Auckland 1310, New Zealand
(a division of Pearson New Zealand Ltd)
Penguin Books (South Africa) (Pty) Ltd, 24 Sturdee Avenue, Rosebank, Johannesburg 2196, South Africa

Penguin Books Ltd, Registered Offices: 80 Strand, London WC2R 0RL, England

www.penguin.com

First published by Michael Joseph 1993
Published in Penguin Books 1994
This re-set edition published 2006
4

Copyright © Nigel Slater, 1993
All rights reserved

The moral right of the author has been asserted

Set in 9.25/13.75 pt PostScript TheSans Light
Typeset by Rowland Phototypesetting Ltd, Bury St Edmunds, Suffolk
Printed in Great Britain by Clays Ltd, St Ives plc

ISBN-13: 978-0-140-23283-7

For Digger, Mr Magrath and Poppy

Contents

Introduction

This is not a book of instant indulgences. *Real Fast Puddings* is simply a collection of ways in which you might like to end your meal, most of which take very little time to prepare. Some are literally instant (it takes just seconds to drop a few velvety raspberries into a glass of chilled Gewürztraminer), while others take a full half hour. This book aims to do nothing more than than show you what wonderful ways there are to finish a meal, some of which you might not have thought of.

I believe passionately that everyone should allow themselves just an hour a day in which to make themselves something good to eat. If they can share what they make with someone, then even better. But it is not always realistic to ask even that, which is why there were some ten-minute main courses in my last book, and even more ten-minute puddings in this one.

I find it more and more difficult to finish my meals on a savoury note. I will happily eat a piece of cheese to finish off the wine, but a morsel of something sweet, perhaps just a mouthful of vanilla ice cream and a liquor-soaked prune or a crisp water biscuit topped with tart berries and sweet clotted cream, is nigh on essential. I am not alone. Almost every letter I received after the publication of *Real Fast Food*, to which this is the companion volume, suggested that I had successfully enticed people back into the kitchen only to abandon them when it came to the pudding stage. This book is not a guide to tarting up instant puddings from a packet or 'a hundred ways with an Arctic Roll'. Neither will it let you get away with custard powder or 'Quick Gel'. The whole point of setting down the hundred, no, two hundred, or so ideas is to show that real food, by which I mean fresh food simply prepared at home with love, need not stop with the main course just because time is not on your side. And when is it?

Imagine a fig bulging with ripe scarlet seeds or a slice of perfect, luscious pear with a piece of grainy Parmesan cheese, or perhaps a thin, crisp apple toast hot from the oven. Consider blackberries steeped in a glass of rich red Barolo or a dish of creamy rice scented with rosewater and pistachios. All these are fast puddings. All of them are light years away from the instant puddings in packets, tins or powders. And most take less of your time than the average ready-prepared pudding takes to reheat or a frozen cheesecake takes to thaw.

Friends always expect a pudding when they come round to supper. On the occasions I have ended the meal with cheese there have been looks of barely concealed disappointment that I haven't produced a dish of boozy trifle or even a pancake with sugar and lemon. Many of the recipes here will prove suitable for entertaining, though most are meant to liven up the daily meal.

I will have no truck with those spoilsports who suggest that puddings are unhealthy. Of course, any form of over-indulgent eating is unacceptable nowadays, but you will find no suggestion in these pages that a rib-sticking treacle pudding or a creamy dessert should be an everyday affair. It should be noted that the backbone of the book is fruit. I find it difficult to think of a day in which fruit in some form is not consumed in my house. In summer it may be berries squashed and stirred into yoghurt as a quick form of fool, or in winter an almond-topped crumble. Here you will find fruit in abundance: roasted, grilled, puréed, baked and brûléed. And I make no apologies for it.

Many of the suggestions are simply classics with their corners cut. A bread and butter pudding made with fruity, buttery *panettone* rather than laboriously buttered white bread, a summer pudding made without the traditional overnight wait or a *tiramisu* that seems none the worse from forgoing its usual chilling time. Whatever quick ways you use, the most important considerations are flavour and pleasure.

A FEW POINTS

Ripeness

I bang on about ripeness all the time. It will probably drive you quite mad. But in fruits, as in cheese or game, ripeness is all. The difference between a fragrant, meltingly soft pear that dribbles juice down your chin and a hard, grainy pear is that one is begging you to eat it, the other not. A truly ripe mango is a gift from heaven, so is a plate of pineapple slices caught just in time, though both are ludicrously juicy to eat. An unripe apple will keep its aromatic subtlety all to itself, apart from giving you tummy ache.

The point at which fruit is ready can be subjective, though generally I insist that nothing is ready unless you can smell it from six inches away. An underripe melon is not worth eating, yet I prefer a slightly firm banana, and an underripe blackberry will still have the welcome trace of acidity now lost in the cultivated ones. But for me, much of the point in eating fruit of any kind is its juice. The more fragrant and sweet the better. It's what makes fruit sexy.

Choosing fruit at its best takes a little care, and I have offered as many clues as I can throughout the book to guide you to picking out the best. Better one fat fig at its brief moment of perfect ripeness than a hundred slices of Black Forest Gâteau.

'I've No Time to Make Puddings'

You don't need half an hour to scatter a few fresh basil leaves over a bowl of strawberries. And it takes barely five minutes to slice a ripe pineapple and sprinkle it with Kirsch. Pan-fried apples with *crème fraîche* can be yours in ten minutes, while even banana custard made with proper custard takes little more than fifteen. So don't talk such rubbish.

'I Can't Afford to Make Puddings'

I feel very strongly about this one. No matter how hard the stores try to keep prices down, and no matter how carefully I shop, I never cease to be amazed at the bill at the checkout. I do not have a fortune to spend on food, though I will admit things are getting better. I have deliberately avoided expensive ingredients, unnecessary lavishness or wastefulness. But not at the expense of flavour. There is no more than a handful of expensive recipes in the book unless, that is, you buy your raspberries out of season and in Knightsbridge. But that is another matter.

Real Fast Food

Real Fast Food is a collection of some 350 ideas for things to cook when you are in a hurry to eat. It was the book that spawned *Real Fast Puddings*, so if you don't have a copy then I suggest you go out and buy one as this second book will then make much more sense. And I will have sold another book.

Speeding up Your Cooking

I have written on this at length in the above, but there are one or two points that are particularly pertinent to puddings.

I am a great believer in cutting corners. Who wants their daily cooking to resemble an exam at cookery school? Not that I would ever put cookery schools down, I think they are wonderful things. I just don't want to run my life like one.

I assume that you have bought this book simply because you want to make your family, your friends, or yourself something nice to eat when you come home, but have very little time or inclination to do so. I will not assume that you want to run around whirling dervish style at seven o'clock at night. The style here is laid back, to say the least. You will find that most of the recipes offer much flavour for exceedingly little work. That is the whole point of the book.

Planning and Precooking

You won't find much of that in here. I have avoided suggesting you marinate the lemon peel in the brandy before you leave for work in the morning, superwoman fashion. I know the state I am in when I leave for work in the morning. Marinating lemon peel is not on my agenda. At 8 o'clock of a morning I can't even make the bed let alone grate a lemon.

Neither will I assume you have a deep freeze big enough to freeze a side of beef. Or that you are the sort of person who has the time or inclination to have fanatically labelled pre-baked tart shells in the freezer. I don't actually have one, unless you count the box at the top of the fridge; and that is packed full with just one bag of coffee beans, a tub of vanilla ice cream and a couple of slabs of puff pastry. There are also a couple of ice-cube trays that smell ever-so-slightly of the cats' fish that was once in there, and badly need replacing. And that is when it hasn't frozen up to the point when I could barely post a letter through it.

Calories

Many people are concerned about their calorie intake, and often tend to avoid eating desserts and puddings as a result. I have found that almost anything marked 'low in calories' also means 'low in flavour'. It seems sad that this should be the case, but it is. For my money, I would rather eat two spoonfuls of something truly delicious but high in calories and fat, say Mascarpone cheese with apricot and almonds, than an entire low-calorie, low-fat cheesecake.

That said, I have included hundreds of suggestions for desserts that contain very few of the dreaded things at all and that will fit neatly into any diet where calories are being counted. Although I remain convinced that a combination of more exercise and smaller portions of delicious food is probably better for you in the long run than getting het up and stressed-out every time you feel like a ball of ice cream.

Sugar

I use sugar in this book. With one or two exceptions I only use sugar where it actually improves the flavour of something. The exceptions generally concern texture or quite simply making something work. I would like to say that strawberries are better without a minute sprinkling of sugar, but they rarely are, or that a little of the deadly white stuff is not really necessary on a pancake, but it is.

For the most part I use unrefined caster sugar, Billington's actually, though I still use the white stuff from time to time, especially if I am making caramel. (Tricky stuff, caramel.) Artificial sweeteners are quite disgusting, leaving an aftertaste in the mouth that only the palate-dead cannot detect. Honey is not always a suitable substitute, and I find brown sugars such as demerara have a bullying, pervasive flavour that is rarely complementary to the recipe. You can take it, though, that if it has been possible to leave it out then I have, but where the battle has been between not using sugar and losing flavour then I am afraid flavour has won.

Butter and Margarine

It is butter every time. I will not have margarine in my house. Anything made with margarine leaves a greasy coating on the roof of one's mouth, akin to a mouthful of Vaseline. No, sorry, it has to be butter. And when I say butter, you can take it that I mean unsalted.

Cream

I use single, double, clotted cream and *crème fraîche* in some of the recipes and suggest them as accompaniments to several of the dishes. I am aware that many people are concerned about their intake of dairy products, particularly of the high-fat ones such as heavy creams. As I have said before, I am not advocating a cream-rich pudding every night, and like most things I suppose that that boring old chestnut 'in moderation' must apply here too. I could also point out, though, that the French have one of the lowest rates of heart attacks in the world. And we all know how they like their dairy produce.

The finest quality cream is creamy-yellow in colour and has a slight acidity. It has a wonderfully rich flavour and is almost without exception the product of smaller dairies. In much the same way that people who have been brought up on woolly, insipid, factory-farmed chicken find free-range birds a bit 'gamey' (all chicken *used* to taste that way), those who have tasted only thin, sterilised creams may actually think real cream tastes slightly 'off'.

Avoid any cream marked UHT. This is cream which has undergone an Ultra Heat Treatment designed to give it a longer shelf-life. Cream that has suffered this process will have almost no flavour at all, will be white or pale grey in colour and extremely thin. I wouldn't give it to the cat.

Single cream, which contains too little butterfat to allow it to thicken when whipped, is fine for accompanying fruit salads and in coffee. Though I have to say I rarely use it.

Double cream is the one suitable for most cooking. It is also the one for whipping. It is easier to overwhip cream than to get it right. Whipped cream should be thick enough to form drifts, but not so stiff that it will stand in peaks. If it looks yellow and grainy then it has gone too far. The trick with whipping cream is to use chilled cream and a cold, dry bowl. The pudding basin that you have rinsed in hot water and shaken dry will almost certainly help your cream to curdle. If using an electric whisk use a medium speed. The fast one is difficult to control, especially as the cream thickens, and if you use the slow setting you will be there all night. As a general rule, stop just before you think it is thick enough, then finish the job with a hand whisk. One more thing to wash up, but better than a bowlful of butter.

Crème fraîche Wonderful stuff. A peculiarly rich cream, popular in France and now gaining weight over here. The joy of the thick, spoonable yellow cream is its slight piquancy, which stops it from cloying, and its absurdly rich texture.

Clotted cream I rather like clotted cream, thick, rich and yellow underneath a thin, slightly crisp skin. Most of it comes from Devon and

Cornwall, and is sold in cute wax cartons or little plastic pots. Known internationally as *the* accompaniment to scones and jam, a spoonful is quite sublime with fruit tarts or eaten off the same spoon as a juicy prune. It is sad that it has gone out of fashion and you now really have to search for it. You can blame the calorie counters for that. No one should have told them it contains almost 200 calories per ounce.

A word about **'whipping' cream** Some may have more luck with this product than I do, but I find that after a little while it starts to slide back into liquid cream, and if used for a *brûlée*, tends to 'fall' when the hot caramel is poured on. No doubt this is because it contains less butterfat than double cream.

Sweetened whipped cream There are several brands of ready-whipped cream on the market. It is mostly sold in aerosol cans, and contains a great deal of air and sugar. It tastes like soap.

Extra thick double cream Some supermarkets, the posh ones, are selling something called 'extra thick' cream. It is meant to be used at the side of the plate, as an accompaniment, rather than for cooking or whipping. I find that it has a 'boiled' flavour, similar to sterilised milk, and prefer to use *crème fraîche* . . .

Flour

This is not a baking book, so there is very little flour used in the recipes. I use white in preference to brown. Use wholemeal instead if you wish, but don't blame me if your pastry tastes like an old cardboard box.

Eggs

All the recipes have been tested using size 2 eggs. I can't think of any recipes in the book so delicately tuned that they will end in tears if your eggs are a size smaller or larger. This is not *haute cuisine*.

I remain a devotee of the free-range egg. I will use nothing else. I have seen for myself how hens are kept in battery cages, and found the whole egg production process positively distressing. I urge anyone with even the remotest conscience to buy free-range eggs. They taste better, anyway.

Chocolate

I also have strong feelings about chocolate, and particularly about the confusion that is permitted to reign between 'candy'-style chocolate and the real stuff. I go into it in more detail in the chocolate section, but will say here that the slabs of pale, soft, sweet 'chocolate' with household names have no place in this book.

THE STORECUPBOARD

A bare cupboard is not much use when you fancy a pudding. Even an egg or two and a pot of decent jam will do, then at least you can have a fluffy, fruity sweet omelette. I list below a few oddments that I have found rather useful on days when I have failed yet again to come home with a handful of perfectly ripe figs or a slice of almond cake from the posh patisserie. Or perhaps I have, but still need a little something to make them special.

Lemons

For stopping cut fruit discolouring and for perking up almost anything. Particularly tropical fruits. An ex-editor friend of mine once told me 'even a tart has half a lemon in her fridge'. I am not quite sure what she meant by 'even'. When you need to use lemon zest, try and buy organic or unwaxed lemons that have not been covered in insecticide.

Citrus Peel

Huge crescent moons of orange, lemon and citron peel for serving with coffee, or slicing and dipping into melted dark chocolate. Available from Italian delis.

Dried Figs, Raisins and Prunes

Instant puddings, look spectacular when piled high on platters.

Tinned Figs

Green, in syrup.

Pistachios

Tantalisingly salty, dusty nuts blushed with purple, beige and green. Bought in large packets in their shells, you may find they vaguely resemble the savoury, addictive nuts you had on holiday. Bought ready-shelled, you might as well eat peanuts. The best seem to come from Lebanese shops, in large, unlabelled plastic bags. Generally speaking, the plumper the nut, the better the flavour. Shelling the little nuts after a soak in the bath will make your fingernails fray.

Almonds

Difficult nuts these. The best-tasting almonds are usually ones that you have shelled yourself, though how you break into the things is quite beyond me. If serving nuts for dessert it will be the almonds that are left when you clear away. Few can crack them. For cooking, ready-shelled ones should really be bought unskinned, and from a shop with a high turnover. But skinning almonds is a drag at the best of times, and totally unsuitable in a book of fast food. Ground almonds are often best bought whole and unskinned, then ground in a blender, skin and all. That way they will be moist, unlike the majority of ground almonds in packets at the grocers.

Crystallised Violets and Rose Petals

The real thing, with a petal inside and not the imitation ones made of icing sugar and colouring in little drums. Try smart chocolate shops or food halls.

Rosewater and Orange Flower Water

Made from the distillation of rose petals and orange blossom. The soft romantic fragrances add a magical perfume to fruits, creams and syrups. Middle Eastern brands are best, though Crabtree and Evelyn do a very fine rosewater, and by post too. Avoid the little bottles in chemists that are rarely strong enough, and instead stock up when you are next in a Turkish deli or Middle Eastern grocers – most major cities have at least one. London has several. Again, you tend to get what you pay for, so go for broke.

Turkish Delight

The best I have ever eaten came from Istanbul via a friend who had been on a shopping trip. Chewy in the extreme and full of pistachios or scented with orange flower or rosewater, I am virtually addicted to the stuff, late at night with little cups of strong coffee.

Marrons Glacés

For solitary moments of wanton extravagance.

A Tube of Smarties

For sandwiches, made with white bread and a thin spreading of butter. Some people (they are usually rather Grand) claim not to like a handful of Smarties. I think they are lying.

Marshmallows

For toasting.

Honey

Again, you tend to get what you pay for. Cheap honey tastes of nothing but sugar – no flowery or herby notes, just sugar. Choose a herby honey, such as thyme or lavender, for recipes involving figs and prunes. And a flower one – orange blossom is the most accessible – for everything else. Runny honeys are generally easier to work with, though set ones are best for spreading on bread and butter soldiers. Farm shops are a good source, or bring a few jars back from holiday.

Jams and Jellies

Even the best jams are not expensive. French-made conserves thick with fruit and very little sugar are good enough to eat straight from the spoon. Greengage, apricot, damson and fig are my all-time favourites. French redcurrant jellies are useful too, but make sure that the redcurrant is crystal clear, runny rather than set, and French. The well-known British versions taste of nothing but sugar and are as stiff as boards. Turkish rose petal jam is good for spooning on to water biscuits with thick yoghurt, and for dunking almond biscuits into. It can be bought from Middle Eastern shops and posh food emporiums. Cherry jam, providing it is made from the tart little morellos and not those candy-flavoured black jobbies, is just the job for eating with *fromage blanc*. In alternate spoonfuls, straight from the pot.

Condensed Milk
Boiled in its tin till thick. For serious sugar attacks.

Vanilla Beans
Actually the fruit of an orchid, sticky, dark vanilla pods give a softer, purer fragrance than even the best essences. But they take a while to give up their flavour to creams and custards so it is best to keep them in a jar of white sugar; the beans will scent the sugar, which can be used in or on almost anything. You can keep good beans for ages in a jar, continually topping the sugar up as you use it. Once they have lost their clout, throw them out.

Vanilla Essence
If you have a bottle of vanilla essence, or anything labelled vanilla flavouring or vanillin, throw it out, then go to a posh food shop and buy . . .

Vanilla Extract
Lacking the nasty chemical taste of the 'essence', vanilla extract is basically made from vanilla beans soaked in an alcohol/water solution. American or French brands are generally better than British. If you have never bought the real stuff before you may be shocked at what you will be asked to pay for it. It's worth it, and lasts for ages, tightly stoppered.

Cocoa Powder
Go for broke. Order the real thing from The Chocolate Society, Barr Lane, Roecliffe, Boroughbridge, North Yorkshire, or buy from smart food shops. Drinking chocolate will not do. For anything. If you are not blessed with a good deli then settle for Van Houten's, which is not too difficult to find.

Spices

Fennel seeds, cinnamon (sticks and ground), nutmeg (whole), coriander seeds and a few whole cloves.

Peppercorns

For bringing out the flavour of strawberries. Keep them whole till you need them to preserve their elusive aromatic warmth.

Balsamic Vinegar

For sprinkling in minute amounts over berries. Put it at the top of your Christmas list or treat yourself to a bottle, even if it is not the best. Who cares, its mellow richness will still do wonders for your berries.

Bath Olivers and Carr's Miniature Water Biscuits

Suitably bland vehicles for delicate jams and jellies and soft cheeses. Ideal companions for quince jelly and thick cream or rose petal jam and *fromage frais*. Try water biscuits heaped with spoonfuls of black-currant conserve and clotted cream and Bath Olivers with figs and goat's cheese.

Ratafia Biscuits

Almondy biscuits in the form of little round ratafias, sponge fingers, or crunchy sugar-coated *amaretti* are enormously useful to have. In pudding emergencies I have served the diminutive almondy cookies alongside coffee cups of melted bitter chocolate for dipping. A memorable success made from an otherwise empty cupboard.

Some Short Cuts

Frozen Puff Pastry, wonderful. Even smart restaurants use it, though they probably won't admit it

Frozen Shortcrust Pastry, less successful; it is just not buttery enough

Meringue Shells, bought ones from the baker or smart pastry shops can be good. Boxed ones in the supermarket tend to be dry and powdery. The centre must be chewy if they are to be any good

Chocolate Cups, I rarely use these, it's not really my style, but friends swear by these ready-made miniature chocolate cases. I might be tempted if the chocolate were better quality

Chocolate Sauce, there are one or two brands of very fine ready-made chocolate sauce. I shall name names: Charbonnel et Walker is the one you want. Though others might be as good. The sexiest sauce I have ever eaten comes in fat glass tubs from the better delis and chocolate shops. I keep a pot of it in the fridge for accompanying ice creams and fruits such as poached pears. Fearfully expensive at first glance, it goes a long way and can be kept in the fridge for a little while and reheated in a few minutes. It is probably the finest convenience food I have come across

Sponge Flan Cases, really quite horrible

Sponge Fingers, a much better choice, even if they are usually as dry as a bone. Great for dipping into fools, and for trifle or *tiramisu*

Tinned Rice Pudding, cold, straight out of the tin, best eaten late at night when seriously drunk

Wafers and Biscuits, Italian and German brands. Fine, if expensive, accompaniments for creams and fools, or for serving with coffee. Only a masochist would make their own *cigarette russe*. Particularly good are those Italian wafer rolls filled with hazelnut and chocolate paste. Find them in delicatessens, by the biscuits

Autumn

blackberries • **plums** • *apples* • **pears** •
chestnuts • **figs** • *the crumble* • **cheeses**

My year is still punctuated by the old school terms, though
I cannot think why. Perhaps it's that I find the beginning
of the calendar year, January and February, so difficult to get
through that I wish the year to have a better start. Autumn is,
without doubt, my favourite season; it's the smell in the air, and
the comfort of lighting the first fire in the hearth.

This is the season of my favourite fruits: dusty, purple-black
damsons; golden greengages; plump, bloomy figs; and the
second flush of blood red, velvety raspberries. Not to mention the
sweet muscat grapes, tart little blackberries and blush-skinned
luscious pears that will end up on the table in some form or
another. This is the time of year when everything seems to be so
ripe as to be nearly alcoholic, that framboise scent that you get
with raspberries or the muscat wine sweetness of Italia grapes.

This is also the season of The Crumble. You can keep your
spotted dicks and jam roly-polys, good rib-sticking things though
they are. For me, the high point of the pudding-maker's year is

when plums, greengages, blackberries and apples are covered in a rough, buttery crumble and served hot from the dish. They can be on the table in half an hour if you make them in not too deep a dish.

This is also the time for pan-frying Cox's Orange Pippins in butter and sugar till caramelised, and serving them with cream. Autumn is for lazy hot puddings like roast figs or grilled pears, a time for baking plums with sweet golden wine and dunking blackberries into glasses of deep red Italian Barolo. The time of year too for matching apples and pears to cheese for the most instant seasonal dessert of all.

I hope you are looking at these recipes because you have been out picking blackberries from the hedgerows and you have a nice basket of them lined with blackberry leaves. These are the best; their flavour intense and their juice copious. Then again you may have picked up a punnet or two from the store on the way home, in which case they will almost certainly be larger, cultivated fruits pampered no doubt by the growers, but their flavour will be more elusive. They will still be good, though, and without the possibility that someone's labrador may have got to them first.

Blackberries Marinated in Cassis

I have said before that I keep very few liqueurs in the house. *Crème de mûres*, which is the very essence of blackberries, is not one of them. But Cassis, the intensely fruity blackcurrant version, has a place on the shelf if only for stirring into glasses of white wine for kir. A quick splash from the Cassis bottle will transform a bowl of purple fruits into the most heady of delights.

Tip the blackberries, which should really be the fleshy cultivated variety this time, into a glass bowl. Pour over a couple of good glugs of Cassis (or *crème de mûres* if you have it) and sprinkle with sugar. Leave to marinate for as long as you can. Serve with a jug of yellow cream.

Blackberries with Fromage Frais *and Cream*

If there are blackberries in season I often unmould a small amount of *fromage frais* into the centre of a plate, scatter a handful of blackberries around it, then pour over a stream of single cream. The effect of the mildly piquant white cheese, the sweet yellow cream and the scent of the purple fruits is positively ambrosial.

Blackberries in Barolo

It doesn't have to be Barolo, but something rich and fruity is called for.

FOR 4

450g / 1lb blackberries
3 tablespoons sugar
300ml / ½ pint Barolo wine

½ cinnamon stick
a long, wide strip of orange zest

Bring the fruit to the boil with the sugar, wine and aromatics in a stainless steel saucepan. Turn down the heat and simmer for 8 minutes. Serve warm or chilled.

Blackberry Gin Sauce

A quick, alcoholic sauce made with juicy blackberries.

FOR 4

225g / 8oz blackberries
75g / 3oz caster sugar

1 tablespoon lemon juice
1 tablespoon gin

Put the fruit into a stainless steel saucepan with the caster sugar, lemon juice and gin. Bring to the boil, then simmer gently for a minute or two. Push through a sieve and serve hot over ice cream or with pancakes.

Blackberries and Cream

Cream, berries and toasted nuts.

FOR 4

100g / 4oz blackberries
2 tablespoons runny honey
1 tablespoon Kirsch
50g / 2oz shelled hazelnuts

150g / 5oz thick, Greek-style
  yoghurt
150ml / ¼ pint double cream

Tip the blackberries into a bowl and pour the honey all over them. Gently stir in the Kirsch. Set aside for 15–20 minutes. Toast the hazelnuts in a frying pan or under the grill. When they are fragrant, rub off some of their papery skins and chop the nuts roughly.

Spoon the blackberries into individual glasses. Mix together the yoghurt and cream. Spoon it over the fruit, cover the cream with chopped hazelnuts and eat with a teaspoon. The cream may curdle slightly where it meets the fruit, but no matter.

Blackberries with Rose Cream and Rose Petals

A romantic, fragrant plate.

Pile blackberries on to individual plates. Flavour pouring-consistency double cream with a little rosewater, then spoon it around the berries. Scatter rose petals from the garden, deep red and fragrant (with their yellow heels snipped off), over the berries. Pass around some almond biscuits such as *amaretti*.

Blackberries with Bay Cream and Almonds

If you are looking for a simple version of one of those piled-high-on-a-big-plate puddings that you get in smart restaurants, here it is. Although they would probably add a little almond biscuit on the side (and no doubt the ubiquitous mint leaf). And so would I. Steeping bay leaves in cream was Sophie Grigson's idea. The rest is mine.

FOR 4

200ml / 7fl oz double cream
1 tablespoon caster sugar
2 bay leaves of a reasonable
  size

2 tablespoons flaked almonds
450g / 1lb blackberries
a little icing sugar

Pour the cream into a small pan and add the sugar and the bay leaves. Bring to the boil, turn the heat very low and simmer, almost imperceptibly, for 8 minutes.

Toast the flaked almonds until they are golden. Pile the berries in the centre of four plates. Pour the bay cream through a sieve then spoon around the berries. Scatter the almonds on top, then dust with a very little icing sugar.

Blackberries and Apples *see also page 58–9*

Can there be a more comforting, feel-good combination of fruits? The very words blackberry and apple have a warm, loving and homely ring about them. Early apples with some tartness to them and sweet little blackberries turn up in all sorts of pies, tarts and puddings, most of which would sit uncomfortably in this collection of fast puddings.

Blackberry and Apple Purée

FOR 3–4
450g / 1lb dessert apples
1 teaspoon ground cinnamon
225g / 8oz blackberries

Core the apples and chop them coarsely. Throw them into a shallow pan, add the spice and a couple of tablespoons of water. Cook over a medium heat, stirring occasionally, till the fruit is soft. This will take about 20 minutes.

Whizz the mixture in a food processor or blender till smooth. But don't overprocess it. Stir in the blackberries, halved if they are particularly large. Stir with a fork so that their juice will stain the purée.

Serve warm, in glasses, with a spoonful of cream or Greek-style yoghurt on top. In which case it may make enough for 4.

Or if you can, leave it to cool, then chill in the fridge. Use as a sauce, perhaps thinned with a little apple juice, for patisserie-bought almond cake, or as a pudding.

Plums *see also page 57–8*

We had plum trees in the garden when I was growing up. Gnarled, bent old trees covered with lichen, just like a story-book orchard. There were deep scarlet and blue-skinned plums with squashy yellow flesh and taller, less rickety greengage trees, which my father called goldengages. When the sun shone you could see through the fruit as far as its stone inside the flesh. The fruit was sweet and juicy and used to smell slightly winy, and the trees were full of large, docile wasps. We made crumbles, pies and some glorious jam.

Now I buy my plums in a transparent plastic carton with a pretty sticker on it and a sell-by date. Six perfect plums sitting on a little sheet of bubble-wrap, as if they were Fabergé eggs. At the height of the season, though, there are wooden crates of the things in my local street market. Red plums, purple plums, dusty damsons with yellow leaves and, occasionally, greengages. When I can shop during the day, I buy the loose fruit from the market, though more often than not I have to shop on the way home from work. Then it's the Fabergé eggs.

A Platter of Plums

Plums come in all sizes and shades. A brilliant harlequin-coloured dessert can be made by piling an assortment of plums, scarlet and blue, orange and gold, purple and yellow-green, on a large white platter. The plums should be ripe but far from squashy, perhaps just dribbling a hint of juice from their stems. Place them in the centre of the table and let everyone help themselves. A glass of something golden and sweet would make the picture even prettier.

Plums with Honey and Crumbs

Too many times have I brought plums home to find them less sweet than they looked. Here is the answer, based on an idea of Margaret

Costa's. Wonderful, incidentally, with damsons, though the stones may annoy.

FOR 4

700g / 1½lb ripe plums	4 tablespoons runny honey
150g / 5oz fresh white or brown breadcrumbs, not too fine	50g / 2oz butter, melted
	2 tablespoons brown sugar

Cut the plums in half and pull out the stones, saving as many of the juices as you can by doing the whole thing over a dish. Mix a good half of the breadcrumbs with the honey and make alternate layers of stoned fruit and honeyed crumbs, starting and ending with fruit.

Mix the remaining crumbs with the melted butter. Stir in the sugar and sprinkle the mixture over the fruit. Bake in a preheated oven, 200°C/400°F (gas mark 6), till crisp and golden, about 25 minutes.

Sautéed Plums

You have a bag of ripe plums. You want a hot pudding. You have only 10 minutes.

Rinse the plums under the tap, drop them into a shallow pan set over a medium heat. Sprinkle lightly with sugar. Throw in a generous knob of butter. Slam on the lid. Cook for 8 minutes, or until the plums start to split. Serve hot with a carton of double cream.

Plums Baked in Sauternes

Good with plums of any sort but even better with greengages, when you can find them. The point of this dessert is in the golden, fruity, winy juices that collect in the bottom of the dish and mingle with the cream.

FOR 3

30g / 1oz butter

75g / 3oz caster sugar

12 medium plums

a wineglass of Sauternes or
other sweet wine

single cream, to serve

Rub the butter around the inside of a shallow baking dish, then sprinkle in the sugar. Add the plums and bake for 10 minutes in a preheated oven at 200°C/400°F (gas mark 6).

Tip the dish slightly and baste the plums with any juices in the bottom of the dish. Pour in the wine and return to the oven till the plums are tender and the cooking juices bubbling, about 15–20 minutes depending on the ripeness of the plums.

Eat from deep bowls, with the buttery juices and a jug of single cream.

DAMSONS

I have a soft spot for damsons, no doubt because of childhood memories of picking the little fruits on misty autumn mornings while waiting for the school bus. I cannot resist them when they appear in the shops in September and October, but I rarely have much time to do anything with them that involves pastry or jam-making, and so tend to use them in a compote or crumble.

Hard, dusty, purple-blue damsons can be turned into a richly coloured, intensely flavoured compote in 20 minutes or so. I know of no other fruit that can be transformed so magically by a few minutes' cooking.

Hot Damson Compote

Remove the little stalks from the fruit, discarding any squashed ones. Put them in a saucepan, stainless steel for preference, and add a small amount of water to come no further than a third of the way up the sides of the pan, and a generous quantity of sugar. Bring quickly to the boil, turn down the heat and simmer gently till the fruits have burst their skins and the juices have worked with the sugar to produce a rich purple sauce, about 15 minutes. Serve hot with cream.

* Upend a measure of gin, or slightly less, into the compote as you bring it to the table. Stir gently

APPLES   *see also page 20*

If you have an apple in the fruit bowl then you have a real fast pudding. It takes but a few minutes to slice and caramelise it with honey and butter, or pan-fry it with vine fruits and Calvados. If it is a truly fine fruit, crisp and aromatic, then it is good enough to eat as it is. Treat it with respect.

The apple is Britain's national fruit. It suits our climate and our taste, and I do think colder climates produce a better-tasting apple. Finding a good apple is easier than it used to be. Many of the large chain stores have taken the lead to encourage growers to plant old-fashioned varieties whose strength is flavour rather than high yield. The response has been encouraging, though many greengrocers have yet to catch on, offering us only a choice of green or red. And both tasteless.

There are warning signs to a tasteless apple. It is usually sold unlabelled. The skin is invariably waxed and shiny. The worst, which is usually deep red, will be oversized and neatly stacked, perhaps even hand polished by a bored assistant. Bite through the tough, greasy skin, and you will find soft, watery flesh, with no detectable apple flavour. The saddest part of all is that these apples are what many of us have been brought up on, and accept uncomplainingly. I should love to force-feed my local supermarket buyer his imported red, insipid apples.

A fine apple, and by fine I mean deeply flavoured, is not difficult to spot. It will probably have a visibly rough skin. It will not shine. Pick it up and sniff it; a tasty apple will generally have a definite scent to it. And it will probably be sold from a wooden crate, though I expect the silly old Eurocrats will have stopped that by now. If you are lucky, your careful choice will be rewarded with old-fashioned apple flavours of strawberry, wine, aniseed or nuts.

AN INCOMPLETE GUIDE TO APPLE VARIETIES

Discovery

The first of the English apples, appearing as early as July, though the later ones in August are often better flavoured. It is possibly my favourite apple; deeply fragrant, a bowlful will scent a warm room within a couple of hours. Discovery are small apples, soft rose and pale green in colour with a crisp white flesh. The flavour is instantly recognisable, with strong raspberry notes. Eat them quickly; they are often gone by October.

Egremont Russet

The best of all the rough-skinned russets, a lovely crisp little apple. It has a rough, browny-yellow skin and a nutty flavour. Not the juiciest variety, but a perfect 'cheese apple'. Best in October and November.

Cox's Orange Pippin

The most famous apple of all, and justly so. A fine choice to offer for dessert, having a wonderful, nutty, aromatic flavour and plenty of juice. It is one of the most highly scented apples, and is also a treat to cook with, keeping more of its rich character than other varieties. Good from December through to March.

Golden Delicious

I hate this apple. I suspect I am probably alone in this. Even Jane Grigson, whose taste in such matters was probably unquestionable, thought 'if you keep it until it is yellow, it is not so bad'. Well, I cannot even have the wretched watery things in the house; I don't even care for the smell, which reminds me of school outings when they were the ubiquitous packed lunch filler. The French should keep them to themselves.

Orléans Reinette

Perhaps the finest-tasting apple in the world. A beautiful, golden orange fruit, larger than most with a golden flesh and copious amounts of juice. Orléans often appears with a little fabric sticker on it, proclaiming its identity with pride. I like to think of it as the French answer to the Cox's, rich and beautifully balanced and available at the same time. Eat such fruit unadulterated, for dessert.

Blenheim Orange

Although in the shops in October, some say that this apple is best later in the year when it has had time to ripen fully. A russet skin gives way to a rich, nutty flesh, sometimes described as winy. The apple has a grainy, open texture that I rather like, though it is inclined to be less juicy than some. I have read that this apple is best at room temperature (see page 28), even slightly warm, though I can't honestly say I have noticed any difference.

Granny Smith

A great many people swear by these green (occasionally blushed), shiny-skinned apples. Better cooks than I extol their virtues for both dessert eating and cooking, though I cannot see what all the fuss is about. To my mind, the Granny Smith is a perfectly serviceable fruit, juicy and mildly flavoured, but nothing to write home about. It has the benefit of being extremely reliable and keeps well; in fact, it can be in fine condition to early spring. Imports, mostly from New Zealand, keep it in stock throughout the year.

OTHER LESS POPULAR VARIETIES TO LOOK OUT FOR

Ellison's Orange

Derivative of Cox's Orange with a distinctive aniseed flavour. Another good apple for cheese. In season from August to October.

Worcester Pearmain

Definite strawberry flavour. An early fruit.

James Grieve

Appears in September, slightly sharp flavour and what some describe as a marrow-like flesh.

Laxton's Fortune

A modern apple from Cox's Orange. It has pretty orangey stripes and a sweet flavour, though I dislike its slightly greasy skin. And, of course, I eat the skin. It has an early season, from July to August.

EATING DESSERT APPLES

The best way to eat an apple is not necessarily straight from the tree. Some apples, Cox's for instance, are often better having been stored for a while. The flavour mellows and you end up with a richer bite. Discovery apples with their clean white flesh and deep fragrance are best eaten as soon as possible.

Munch them in the hand by all means, but a really fine apple deserves a plate and a little knife, if not a linen napkin. You may find an apple's flavour is more pronounced when eaten at room temperature; there is no real reason to refrigerate them anyway. The fruit should be thoroughly wiped to remove the worst of the wretched insecticides and fungicides used nowadays.

Pan-fried Apples

Dessert apples, fried in butter till golden, take barely 10 minutes and can be used in all manner of puddings.

FOR 2
scant 50g / 2oz butter
**400g / 14oz dessert apples, cored and chopped into 2.5cm / 1 inch
pieces**

Melt the butter in a shallow pan. Add the apple cubes and cook over a medium to high flame till golden and tender, about 10 minutes. Turn the heat up near the end of cooking to crisp the outsides a little. Remove with a draining spoon.

* Serve the apples hot, surrounded by a pool of cold, fresh cream

* Remove the apples from the pan, add 4 tablespoons of fresh white or brown breadcrumbs and fry in the apple butter till golden. Scatter over the apples and eat while hot

* Stuff the hot apples into a pancake (page 35–6) and roll it up

* Add a tablespoon of runny honey towards the end of cooking, then eat the sweet result with a side dish of cold thick yoghurt

* Make an omelette as on page 100, using the apples as an alternative filling

Croissants with Hot Apples and Crème Fraîche

Minute for minute, probably the most delicious fast pudding in the book.

FOR 2

30g / 1oz butter
1 large dessert apple
2 tablespoons caster sugar

2 large, flaky croissants
3 tablespoons crème fraîche

Melt the butter in a shallow pan. Halve and core the apple and cut into about ten segments. Cook the apple in the butter till tender, turning once to cook the other side, then add the sugar and cook over a high heat till the mixture caramelises.

Warm the croissants under the grill, split each one in half, and sandwich together with the crème fraîche and some of the hot apple slices. Spoon over any remaining buttery sauce, and replace the top halves. Eat while still hot.

* Good though the matching of crumbly, flaking croissant with hot sticky apples and cold, slightly soured cream is, you may want to gild the lily. Try a spoonful of proper jam, something with a bit more bite to it, such as blueberry or gooseberry, tucked inside with the apple. The jam should be high-fruit, low-sugar, and compatible with apple, ie, blackberry or quince rather than raspberry or strawberry

Apples with Caramel Sauce

If the apple you have in the fruit bowl is not tasting as good as it might, turn it into a hot pudding with the addition of just some sugar and butter. Brandy in some form or another will lift this little dish on to a higher plane.

FOR 1

1 large dessert apple	1 tablespoon brandy, preferably
scant 50g / 2oz butter	Calvados
2 or 3 tablespoons caster sugar	2 tablespoons double cream

Cut the apple into four from stalk to flower end and remove the core. Melt the butter in a shallow pan. When it starts to sizzle add the apple pieces and turn down the heat. Cook the apples slowly until tender, taking care that the butter does not burn. Remove the apples with a slotted spoon to a warm plate.

Sprinkle in the sugar, the amount depending on how sweet you want your sauce to be. Let the butter and sugar caramelise and start to turn golden. Add a tablespoon of Calvados and two of double cream. Allow the sauce to bubble for a minute, then spoon it over the apples. You may have a little too much sauce. You can always dunk your bread in it.

Apple Toasts with Apricot Caramel Cream

This slightly more substantial version of the previous recipe has a stickiness about it that demands sharp *crème fraîche* or thick yoghurt on the side.

FOR EACH PERSON

1 large dessert apple	1 heaped tablespoon apricot jam
40g / 1½oz butter	a squeeze of lemon
2 tablespoons brown (not	1 tablespoon *crème fraîche* or
muscovado) or caster sugar	thick yoghurt
1 round of bread cut from a	
crusty loaf	

Peel and slice the apple into eight pieces and remove the core. Melt the butter in a shallow pan over a medium heat. Add the sugar and when it dissolves tip in the apple pieces and simmer for 8 minutes until tender and fluffy. Take care not to let the sugar and butter burn.

Meanwhile, toast the bread till golden. When the apple is ready, remove from the pan with a draining spoon and put on the hot toast.

Place the apricot jam in the pan, turn up the heat and stir for 1 minute until it has melted into the caramel sauce. Add a squeeze or two of lemon juice, taste and add more if you like. Pour immediately over the apples and toast and eat while hot with a dollop of yoghurt or cream, thick and cold from the fridge.

Grilled Apples

A recipe based on one for pears in Patricia Hegarty's book *An English Flavour*. An inspiring book by a cook who grows almost all her own fruit, vegetables and herbs, including a selection of old-fashioned apples such as the local Worcester Pearmain.

FOR 2

2 dessert apples, Cox's for preference

juice of ½ lemon

30g / 1oz butter, melted

1 tablespoon runny honey

Peel the apples and halve them from stalk to flower end. Cut out the core. Brush all over with lemon juice, then lay the fruit down flat on a grill rack. Brush with the butter.

Grill, about 10cm / 4 inches away from the heat, until the apples begin to brown, about 10 minutes. Turn them over, brush with butter and grill until the apples start to colour. Pour the honey into the hollows where the cores were, and return to the grill. When the honey bubbles, and the apples are tender to the point of a knife, they are done. Eat with cream or ice cream.

Apple Purée

A bowl of apple purée is simple enough to make and is a good thing to have around, as a base for quick puddings of all sorts.

MAKES ABOUT 350G / 12OZ, OR ABOUT 12 HEAPED TABLESPOONS
500g / 1lb 2 oz dessert or Bramley apples
1 teaspoon cinnamon
½ teaspoon mixed spice

Cut the apples in half, remove the cores and then chop roughly. The pieces can be quite large. Throw them into a shallow pan with the spices and a couple of tablespoons of water (or cider or apple juice if there is some around).

Set the pan over a low to medium heat, shaking or stirring the pan occasionally, and checking that nothing has stuck. Add a little more liquid if it looks as though it needs it; the mixture is done when the apples are reduced to a thick mush, about 20 minutes. Perhaps less.

Whizz in the food processor or blender for a few seconds till smooth. But stop before it turns to baby food.

A Few Things to Do With Apple Purée

* Serve the purée as it is, on a soup plate, stirring in a dollop of thick yoghurt or cream

* Spread on to hot buttered toast for a snack

* Chilled, as a dip for coarse, crisp oatcakes

* As a sauce for a plain almond sponge cake, which you will have bought from a very expensive patisserie on the way home

Apple Yoghurt Fool

FOR 4

the apple purée opposite,
  chilled, sweetened with
  1 tablespoon runny honey

250g / 9oz thick natural
  yoghurt or use ½ yoghurt and
  ½ softly whipped cream

Stir the chilled and sweetened purée into the yoghurt or half yoghurt and cream. Spoon into four wineglasses and leave in the fridge for as long as you can; half an hour would be ideal. Eat with crisp almond biscuits.

* If you want to put something on top I suggest a sprinkling of flaked almonds toasted till golden brown or a scattering of breadcrumbs, cooked in butter till golden and crisp

Apple Snow with Maple Syrup Sauce

FOR 4

150ml / ¼ pint maple syrup
100ml / 4fl oz double cream
75g / 3oz butter

2 large egg whites
½ teaspoon cream of tartar
the apple purée opposite

Place the maple syrup, cream and butter into a small pan and simmer over a medium heat till slightly thickened, stirring from time to time. This will take about 10 minutes. Pour into a cool jug and set aside.

Beat the egg whites with the cream of tartar till they form stiff peaks. Gently and slowly beat in the apple purée, a little at a time. The mixture should be soft enough to hold its shape in a spoon.

Divide the mixture between four wineglasses. Chill till required. When you are ready to eat, stir the maple syrup sauce, and spoon some of it over the apple snow. You may have too much. It will keep, refrigerated, for a couple of days.

Golden, Fragrant Baked Apples

This version of baked apples is a finer thing altogether than the usual Bramleys stuffed with mincemeat, which are too often watery and oversweet, not to mention overlarge. Choose large dessert apples – something aromatic such as Cox's would be perfect – and you will have fluffy golden globes within the half hour. One of my favourite recipes in the book.

FOR 2

2 large Cox's Orange Pippins
2 walnut-sized knobs of butter
juice of 1 orange

1 juicy passion fruit (lightly wrinkled and heavy for its size)

Heat the oven to 220°C/425°F (gas mark 7). Core the apples with an apple corer or small knife. Cut a line around the circumference of the apple, just deep enough to pierce the skin. Place in a small flat dish and put a knob of butter in each cavity. Squeeze over the orange juice and put in the hot oven.

Bake for 25 minutes till the skin is golden and the fruit is puffed up and fluffy. Remove from the oven and immediately squeeze half a passion fruit over each apple, seeds and all. Eat while the apples are still hot and deeply fragrant from the butter, orange and passion fruit.

Quick Apple Tarts

These little tarts take a matter of minutes to make. They are at their best when cooked slightly more than you would think, so that the pastry is very crisp and the apples lightly caramelised. I usually eat these with thick, yellow cream.

FOR 2

150g / 5oz ready-made puff pastry
2 medium apples, peeled and cored
30g / 1oz butter, melted

1 tablespoon sugar
2 tablespoons apricot, green-gage or fig jam, warmed

Preheat the oven to 220°C/425°F (gas mark 7). Put a baking sheet into the oven to heat. (The point of this is to ensure that the bottom of the tarts is cooked thoroughly.) Cut the pastry in half and roll out each square large enough to cut a circle of pastry about 16cm / 6½ inches. That's about the size of a side plate. Cut out two discs of pastry using a side plate as a template.

Slice the apples thinly. Prick the pastry four or five times to stop it puffing up and tossing the apples on to the baking sheet. Place the apples, neatly if you have time, on the pastry, leaving a clear edge of about 2.5cm / 1 inch. Brush the apples and the pastry with butter without letting the butter drizzle down the sides of the pastry, which may prevent it rising.

Sprinkle over the sugar and transfer the tarts to the hot baking sheet. The easiest way to do this is to remove the baking sheet from the oven and lift on each tart using a fish slice, plus a bit of help from your fingers. Leave as much space on the sheet between the tarts as possible. Bake for 15 minutes. Remove the tray from the oven and pour over the warmed jam. Return to the oven for 4 or 5 minutes till the jam is bubbling, the pastry crisp and the apples slightly browned at the edges.

Apple Pancakes

If you have eggs in the kitchen and apples in the fruit bowl then you have a real fast pudding.

FOR 4

100g / 4oz plain flour
salt
1 tablespoon caster sugar
3 eggs
225ml / 8fl oz milk

4 small dessert apples
knob of butter, melted
butter, for frying
sugar, for sprinkling

Whizz the flour, salt, sugar, eggs and milk in the blender or food processor till smooth. A matter of seconds. Whisk them together by hand if you prefer. The resulting batter should be the same consistency as double cream. Add a little water if it is too thick. Set aside for as near to 30 minutes as you can. Ten will do.

Remove the cores from the apples. An apple corer will help, though you can use a long bladed small knife if you can't find the corer. (It will be at the very back of the drawer, with the rusty piping nozzles.) Slice the apples into thin rounds.

Stir a knob of butter, melted or very soft, into the batter. Melt a little butter in a suitable pan. I cook pancakes in my omelette pan, which is now so old and seasoned that I can even scrub it clean and it rarely sticks. Ideally, it should be about 20cm / 8 inches in diameter and with slightly turned up edges. A frying pan will be fine as long as you know it doesn't stick.

When the butter sizzles, pour out any that is more than just a thin coating, then pour in enough batter to coat the bottom thinly. It does not matter if the pancake has a few holes; in fact, I regard them as something of a plus. (There are very detailed pancake directions on page 102–3.) As the batter starts to cook, add a few of the apple rings in a single layer. Pour over more batter to cover the apples and cook for a minute till lightly set.

Turn the pancake over. This is easy enough to do with a large flat fish slice, though I always use my fingers as well. Flipping it over quickly has always proved more successful for me than dithering about, expecting it to break. Cook the remaining side and serve warm, sprinkled with a little sugar. Repeat with the other apples and the remaining batter.

Praline Ice Cream with Hot Apples, Honey and Spices

I love puddings that marry the blisteringly hot with the icy cold. Vanilla ice cream with hot chocolate sauce is one, this fruity sauce, which smells like baked apples, another. A nutty ice cream, such as walnut or almond-rich praline, would not be too much here, though vanilla would be fine. The ice cream should be very cold.

400g / 14oz dessert apples

scant 50g / 2oz butter

3 tablespoons runny honey

pinch of ground cinnamon

pinch of mixed spice

75g / 3oz large juicy raisins

vanilla or praline ice cream for 2

Cut the apples, it will probably be about two large ones, into four. Take out the cores and cut each piece of apple into chunks. Melt the butter with the honey in a shallow pan. Add the spices. Leave the sauce to bubble over a medium heat for a minute or so, stirring occasionally. Add the apples and raisins.

Turn the heat so that the apples are just simmering. Cook for 7–10 minutes till they are tender. Place a large ball of ice cream on each plate, then spoon around the hot fruit. Pour the bubbling sauce over the ice cream and eat immediately to make the most of the startling contrast in texture.

Pan-fried Apple and Cheshire Cheese Savoury

FOR 2

1 large or 2 small dessert apples

juice of ½ lemon

1 tablespoon walnut oil

2 tablespoons shelled walnuts

a handful of salad leaves such as chicory

75g / 3oz Cheshire cheese

Wipe the apples but don't bother peeling them. Cut them in half and then into quarters. Remove the cores and cut each apple into thick slices, probably about eight per apple. Squeeze a little lemon juice on to the flesh to stop it discolouring.

Warm the oil in a shallow pan, place the apple slices in the pan and scatter over the walnuts. Cook over a medium heat until the apples are golden and tender and the walnuts are fragrant, about 5 minutes, turning them once. Place a few salad leaves on each of two plates. Remove the apples with a palette knife and place on top of the leaves.

Crumble the cheese into small lumps, about the size of walnut halves, and scatter immediately over the hot apples. The cheese will soften slightly. Pour any remaining lemon juice into the pan, turn up the heat and scrape any bits stuck on the pan into the dressing. Bubble for a couple of seconds then pour the pan juices (there won't be a lot) over the cheese and apples.

Apples and Cheese

I am convinced that apples and cheese were made for each other. A marriage made in heaven as far as I am concerned. I would even go so far as to suggest that, to my taste, certain cheeses are best with certain apples, and list them below.

Cheddar and Cox's Orange Pippin
The classic English cheese and the classic English apple. Choose something with a bit of clout such as Montgomery's, Quick's (now available in supermarkets too) or Keen's Cheddars and go for a truly ripe Cox's. Good November and December eating.

Taleggio and Discovery
Taleggio is a mild, rather milky Italian cheese of which I am particularly fond. It is standard fare in Italian grocers and cheesemongers, though more difficult to find in chain stores. I particularly like the mild softness of the cheese with the crisp, light, slightly acid flesh of the little Discovery apples. Best to eat while the apples are young.

Cheshire and Egremont Russet
Any russet apple seems to work well with this cheese. Although Egremont Russets are not the juiciest of apples I think they make a good cheese apple. I have a preference for eating them with Mrs Appleby's unpasteurised Cheshires, which are now finding their way to a larger audience thanks to the supermarket buyers. Both cheese and fruit will make good eating right through the autumn and winter.

Wensleydale and Apple Tart
A combination as old as the hills. Although I have found recipes for placing the cheese under the pastry before cooking, I much prefer mine in thin slices on top of the pie. The cheese should be sliced thin enough to cut with a fork and thick enough to be interesting.

PEARS

To finish an autumn supper with a single aromatic pear, golden-skinned and freckly with buttery, juicy flesh, can be a great joy. If the fruit is really fine, it can be eaten for lunch with nothing more than a piece of cheese and some crusty, open-textured bread.

It can be difficult to catch pears at their point of perfection, when they are at their most juicy and sweet. You have to keep an eye on them. Like so many fruits I find it best to buy them slightly underripe and finish them off at home. Although I like the bland crunch of a hard, glassy pear, that is hardly when they are at their best. Most yield more flavour when they are blushed and turning slightly yellow, though it is as well to remember that at this point they bruise as easily as a peach.

In the autumn most shops will offer a couple of varieties of pear; if you are lucky it will be Williams' Bon Chrétien and Doyenne du Comice. Perhaps it will be Conference. In the spring, the most they will offer is hard green fruit from South Africa or New Zealand that ripens to a boring watery sweetness devoid of any aroma.

Comice pears are plump and blunt, greenish-yellow in colour with a red blush. They are one of the sweetest pears and highly fragrant, a perfect dessert fruit. Williams', known as Bartlett in the States, is another fat, rounded pear which turns yellow-blush as it ripens. Conference, the tapered green and russet pear, is probably easiest to find in late autumn and early winter. It has a nutty flavour and a grainy texture that I like very much with cheese.

A Plate of Pears

Choose ripe, juicy pears, Williams' or Comice perhaps. They should be firm enough to be picked up easily when sliced but ripe enough to dribble a little when you peel them. Except you are not going to peel them. Cut the pears in half and in half again, then remove the cores. Place the pear pieces on a white plate: they can be arranged prettily or piled hugger mugger but they should have their fleshy side up, skin side down.

Get out the eau de vie bottle. Poire William would be wonderful, but *framboise*, which is the very essence of crushed raspberries, is surprisingly good here too. Covering most of the open bottle neck with your thumb, sprinkle a little of the heavenly scented liquor over the fruit. Serve slightly chilled.

You may want to rub the cut side of the fruit with half a lemon if you are going to leave the fruit to chill for any length of time.

* I tried this with Calvados, the apple brandy, but the alcohol hid rather than flattered the fruit

* If ever you come across a pear sorbet at one of those posh ice cream shops, then bring it home, eat it in chilled bowls surrounded by slices of pears and Poire William eau de vie

Pears with Almonds or Hazelnuts

A lovely idea from Lynda Brown which takes the pears and Poire William idea slightly further. To the above recipe, if you can call it that, add a handful of toasted almonds or hazelnuts, rubbed in a tea towel to remove their skins, and chopped coarsely.

Pears and Pepper

Try grinding a little black pepper over quarters of ripe pear. Not too much, and not too fine. Just enough to bring out the flavour.

Pears and Peppercorns

Soft green peppercorns, aromatic and a little hot, are sold in grocers and delicatessens in jars of brine. I have taken to crushing a few drained ones with the back of a spoon (say half-a-dozen for each pear) and spreading them somewhat haphazardly over halves of the fruit. More of a snack than a dessert.

A Little Trick with Pears

If you have bought pears that are far from ripe you can bring them to perfection more quickly if you keep them in a paper bag with, and this is not a myth, a ripe apple. Do not seal the bag fully, leave a little hole in the top and put it in a warm, but far from hot, place. The pears will ripen much faster than if left to their own devices.

A Pear Snack

Something to nibble on your own. Wipe and quarter a ripe pear, remove the core, then dip the fruit, each piece as you eat it, into runny, golden honey. Chestnut is my favourite for this, but orange blossom or heather honey can be good too. Give the medicinal euca-lyptus honey a miss.

Baked Pears with Vanilla Ice Cream

Although this buttery, fruity pudding stretches the 30-minute limit to the full, I include it because of its ease of preparation and the delicious way the hot, sweet pear juices mingle with the cold ice cream. Use the very best vanilla ice cream you can buy.

FOR 4

4 large, juicy pears
50g / 2oz caster sugar
1 tablespoon lemon juice
a vanilla pod

50g / 2oz butter, melted
good quality vanilla ice cream,
    straight from the freezer

Peel and core the pears and cut them into thin slices. Toss them into an ovenproof dish with the caster sugar, lemon juice, vanilla pod and melted butter. Level the pears and bake in a preheated oven, 200°C/400°F/(gas mark 6), for about 30 minutes, until tender and golden. A couple of times during cooking, tip the dish slightly and baste the pears with the cooking juices.

Place a scoop of ice cream on each of four plates, surround by some of the hot fruit and spoon some of the rich, buttery juices over the soft, hot pears and the cold, hard ice cream.

A Cream to Serve with Ripe Pears

An idea from a favourite cookery book, *Chez Panisse Cooking* by Alice Waters. Sadly now out of print and mysteriously unavailable in paperback either.

I cannot explain why blackcurrants, normally so bullying and intensely flavoured, flatter pears in the way they do. Here, a liqueur made from the fruit (and one of the few I have knocking around) is folded into a cream to accompany slices of juicy, honey-fleshed pear.

Beat 225ml / 8fl oz double cream till it stands in soft peaks, just short of what you would normally call softly whipped. Fold in a couple of tablespoons of Cassis, the stuff you use in kir, a little at a time and mix slowly until it has scented the cream.

PEARS WITH SOFT CHEESES

Creamy, sweet soft cheeses partner pears perfectly. Mascarpone, the rich and thick Italian cream cheese, or even the white and lumpy cottage cheese from the supermarket can turn a pear into a pudding in minutes. There is something that works for me about the graininess of the pear, and the smoothness of the cheese.

Pears with Mascarpone

Choose ripe, juicy pears and Mascarpone cheese at room temperature. Comice would be perfect for this. Allow one fruit per person,
wipe it and cut it into quarters from core to flower end. Remove the
core, then place on a large plate. Put a dish of Mascarpone cheese in
the centre and let everyone dip their pears in the cheese.

Warm Pears with Melted Mascarpone

FOR 2

2 ripe Comice pears
100g / 4oz Mascarpone cheese

Quarter the pears and core them. Place the fruit, skin side down, in
a shallow heatproof dish. Spoon a dollop of Mascarpone cheese over
each quarter, then place under a preheated medium hot grill till it
melts. Serve while the cheese is still soft and runny.

PEARS AND BLUE CHEESE

Blue-veined cheeses can be just as good with pears as hard Parmesan
and soft cream cheeses. One of my favourite desserts is a ripe,
honey-sweet pear with a slice of Gorgonzola or a lump of Stilton.
When I can afford Roquefort, the French blue cheese with a salty
bite, I often buy pears to enjoy with it at the same time.

Pears with Walnuts and Blue Cheese

I leave the choice of cheese to you. Cashel Blue, the soft and creamy
Irish cheese, or a firmer Colston Bassett Stilton will marry as happily
with pears as a lump of deeply flavoured Gorgonzola. The fastest
way to serve them is to place a large piece of the blue-veined cheese
in the centre of the table with a plate of yellow and blush-pink pears.

Scatter a few whole walnuts around and let everyone sort it out for themselves.

With a little more time you could make individual plates of sliced cheese and wiped, quartered and cored fruit. And you could remove the walnuts from their shells.

Lockets' Savoury

Lockets was one of those masculine Westminster restaurants that served nursery food to Members of Parliament. This was the place to come for asparagus, salmon and strawberries in season. The pudding trolley was, by all accounts, not worth bothering with (when are they?), so diners tended to finish their meals with cheese or something hot from the kitchen. They would then no doubt doze off until woken by the inhouse division bell. Even the 1971 *Good Food Guide* noted it was 'within shuffling distance of the House of Commons'. Lockets' Savoury must have been what they did with the ends of the Stilton.

FOR 2, AS A SAVOURY OR SNACK

2 thickish slices of white bread cut from a decent crusty loaf

a few sprigs of watercress

1 large ripe pear, peeled and cored

freshly ground black pepper

150g / 5oz Stilton cheese

Toast the bread on both sides, then remove the crusts if you want to give the dish a modicum of elegance. Divide the watercress between the two slices of toast. Slice the pear thinly and arrange the fruit on the toast. Season with a little freshly ground pepper. Remove thick shavings of Stilton with a potato peeler and place them over the pear, then place in a preheated hot oven, 200°C/400°F (gas mark 6), till the cheese is melting. Eat warm.

PEARS WITH HARD CHEESES

Pears and Pecorino

Pecorino is an Italian cheese made from sheep's milk, though it is not dissimilar in flavour to a young Parmesan. In Tuscany it is traditionally eaten with pears, at the end of a meal.

Young Pecorino is the one you want to eat as dessert – tell your cheesemonger otherwise he'll sell you the harder, though even tastier, Pecorino Romano. Ask to taste it, it should be not too salty and soft enough to slice with a potato peeler. Buy a fair-sized lump that will last for a couple of meals. Should you fail to use it all quickly enough, it makes a grating cheese almost as good as Parmesan.

Choose pears that are really ripe; hard fruit will ruin this dish. Go by smell, which should be sweet. Use one fruit per person. Wipe the pears but do not peel them. Slice them into quarters from stem to flower end. Slice out the core and set them on a plate, sprinkled with a little lemon juice to keep them from browning.

Using a vegetable peeler, take thick shavings, as large as you can, from the cut side of the cheese and lay these on the plate with the pears. Eat while the pears are still moist.

Let's Take the Idea a Little Further . . .

Pears with Melted Pecorino

As before, the fruit must be really ripe. Use young Parmesan if you prefer.

Halve the pears, core and peel them. Lay each half flat on the bottom of the grill pan. Holding the pear in shape with one hand, cut the pear into thin slices. Cut a slice of Pecorino with a vegetable peeler or sharp knife for each pear half. Lay the cheese over the fruit.

Place under a preheated hot grill until the cheese starts to melt a little (it won't bubble like Cheddar would). As it browns very slightly in patches remove from the heat and lift on to plates using a large flat spatula or fish slice. Eat hot.

... And a Little Further Still ...

Pears with Melted Pecorino and Chestnut Honey

When I first saw this on an Italian restaurant menu I was extremely suspicious, and ordered it out of curiosity.

It is surprisingly delicious, and is, in essence, no different from traditional marriages of savoury and sweet like Cheshire cheese with sweet fruit cake or the Spanish snack of Manchego cheese with quince paste.

FOR EACH PERSON

½ large, very ripe pear
2 large slices of Pecorino or
  Parmesan cheese

1 tablespoon runny honey,
  preferably chestnut
a little icing sugar

Heat the grill. Peel the pear. Halve and core it. Place each half flat down on a grill pan and slice it thinly as in the preceding recipe. Place the cheese slices on the pear, drizzle over the honey and grill till bubbling. Dust very lightly with icing sugar. Eat while still warm.

Pears with Parmesan and Walnuts

I prefer a slightly firmer pear with this savoury, bordering on the pungent, cheese. Young Parmesan cheese can be peeled in large wafers with a vegetable peeler. Even the main stores sell Parmesan at a suitable age for this, though strangely not always the Italian grocers where you might look first.

Wipe the pears, which might be ripe and granular-fleshed Conference, quarter them and remove the cores. I particularly enjoy the slightly rough, dry skin of such a variety, though some may prefer to remove it. Lay the pears on a plate, cut into thinner pieces if you like, and cover with thin wafers, or shavings if your skill with the peeler wasn't up to much, of Parmesan and scatter freshly shelled walnut halves over the cheese.

* If I am eating alone I will just break off a knob of Parmesan and munch it with the pear. In which case I will probably be eating it for lunch rather than as an after-dinner savoury

Hard Pears and Old Parmesan

There is a difference between a firm and a hard pear. Firm pears yield slightly when squeezed and soften after 20 minutes' cooking. Hard pears are made edible only by long poaching in a sweet syrup, possibly containing wine and aromatics. When you bravely bite into them raw their flesh will be hard, white and glassy; there may be flavour but there will be no perfume. Tapered Conference pears are more likely to be hard. They have no real place in this book other than for me to mention that I occasionally buy them just to match their grainy, crisp flesh with a piece of equally grainy and crisp, mature Parmesan. The sort you would usually grate. A deeply savoury combination that makes the veins stand out on the roof of your mouth.

MARRONS GLACÉS

A plate of frosted, mealy *marrons glacés* is a treat indeed. The whole chestnuts are soaked in syrup and dried over and over again until they develop a melting consistency within and a crisp, sugary outer shell. Forget what anyone tells you about them being expensive and disappointing. They are talking rubbish. *Marrons glacés* are a delicacy, in the true sense of the word. And, like all true delicacies, are fearfully, outrageously expensive.

Should you have a surplus of the things (I cannot imagine why) or should you need to make a few stretch a long way, then there are one or two possibilities. Although if I had only a few *marrons glacés* to serve my guests I would give them something else, and wolf the *marrons* myself. In secret.

* Crush the *marrons* with a fork, using, say, one per person. Mix with a tablespoon of softly whipped cream per person and a splash, no more, from the brandy bottle. Spread on tiny, shop-bought meringues or those sugared sponge fingers people use for trifle, but not *amaretti*, which are too strongly flavoured, and eat with coffee. Don't try this for less than four. You cannot whip less than 4 tablespoons of cream successfully. At least, I can't

* Crumble, rather than crush, the *marrons*. Stir them into double cream that has been whipped into thick waves. Set aside for 20 minutes, then spoon in dollops with French fig jam on to thin slices of crackly baguette

CHESTNUT PURÉE

People seem divided over chestnut purée, in much the same way as they are over chicken livers or gooseberries. I have known some go into complete ecstasy over a bowlful, lightly sweetened with icing sugar and topped with whipped cream, sundae-style. Others have likened the stuff to dog food.

Chestnut purée is best made with fresh chestnuts, which you will have peeled yourself. You will probably have shrivelled your fingers in the hot soaking water and torn your nails to shreds too. Your hands will look like something from an Edgar Allan Poe story. Just this once, forget the best for the sake of speed and go for second best. The tinned, unsweetened stuff.

Don't be put off by the dull browny-grey lump. It is just a starting point and needs a little embellishment. Brandy, say, or sherry, meringues, a bit of sugar, thick fluffy cream or perhaps melted chocolate. Though I have known those who can enjoy it straight from the tin.

Chestnut Cream

Mix a tin of chestnut purée with an equal quantity of whipped cream. Easy enough to do if you tip the contents of the tin into a bowl, and mash it into submission with a large fork. Half fill the empty tin with double cream, beat slowly with a fork till thick and almost at the point where it stands in peaks. Fold carefully into the nut purée.

Add a drop or two (I should make it two, at least) of brandy, and stir in. Taste it, and add some icing sugar, if you think it needs it. It probably will. Spoon into glasses and serve with a thin, posh biscuit. One of those cigarette wafers filled with chocolate truffle would be nice.

* Top each glass with shavings of dark chocolate

* Best served in small amounts, it really is rather rich

CHOCOLATE CHESTNUT CREAM

A rather luxurious pudding for a cool late autumn night.

FOR 4

175g / 6oz dark chocolate
350g / 12oz chestnut purée
1 tablespoon icing sugar

225ml / 8fl oz double cream
cocoa powder, to sprinkle

Break the chocolate into pieces and melt in a small bowl over hot water. There are full instructions for melting chocolate in the chocolate section on page 131–2. Crush the chestnut purée with a fork and stir in the icing sugar. Gently stir in the melted chocolate.

Put the chocolate chestnut mixture in the fridge while you whip the cream into soft drifts rather than stiff peaks. Leave the chocolate chestnut mixture for 10 minutes or more if you have time, then spoon into glasses. Top with spoonfuls of whipped cream and sprinkle with cocoa powder. Make sure it's the proper stuff.

* Gild the lily even further by scattering toasted almond flakes on top of the cream

* After a rich main dish this will stretch to 6, if served in small glasses

GRAPES

If anyone tells you that grapes are good when cooked I suggest you treat them with suspicion. Grapes, at least in my house, are to be eaten from the vine, at the table, if not from the bag on the way home. My favourite way to present them is in a bowlful of iced water. Then the fruit gets really cold and the skins get tight and each grape seems to burst when you bite into it, exploding with its sweet juice.

It is the late-season muscat grapes that particularly excite me. Catching them at their peak is easy enough; just let them go very yellow before eating them. That way they will be at their sweetest. Look out for Italia grapes, but eat them only when they are truly golden, there is little pleasure to be had in underripe grapes. Red grapes, often called Flame or some such name, are rarely as good as they look.

From time to time I buy a bunch of big gobstopper black ones, but they have no real flavour. The silly little sour green seedless ones can be fun, though hardly a gastronomic treat. Grapes have a better flavour the nearer they are to rotting.

Figs are perfect for the fast foodie. They respond well to a small amount of heat, their flavour reaching its height when they are warm. Long cooking does them no favours at all.

They are for me one of the finest flavoured fruits, scarlet-fleshed, sensual things that they are. I rank them up there with ripe, cold muscat grapes, raspberries and mulberries, dribbling peaches and perfumed Charentais melons. It is hard to find a fruit that is such a joy to look at, let alone eat.

I have to say I prefer the purple to the green, and the fatter and squatter the better. If they look swollen, sore even, they are probably going to be good to eat; if they look as though they are about to burst and have glistening beads of stickiness from the flower end, then they could be sublime.

Even the names of the varieties are a joy to read: Negronne; Negro Largo; and Violette de Bordeaux. There is one named Madonna. There is no doubting its sexiness, though I have read enough purple prose about fig-eating to excite me for a lifetime.

Figs on Ciabatta

Ciabatta, the open-textured, slipper-shaped Italian bread, provides a chewy base for a snack of figs. Simply break off pieces of the bread and munch them with the ripe figs.

A Few Facts About Figs

* There are few figs that need peeling; the skin is almost always edible

* The heavier the fig, the more succulent it is likely to be

* Figs taste better when they are warm; leave them in the sun before eating if you can

* Figs are totally wasted in a fruit salad

* If you are looking for a cheese to match with figs, then you will do no better than a Brie, preferably on the firm side

* Figs have an affinity with yoghurt, clotted cream, cream cheeses, honey, raspberries (and I would add blackberries), and herbs such as thyme and lavender. Oh, and walnuts

* If I am feeling even lazier than usual, I will sometimes tear a fig in half, spread on a small amount of cream or cottage cheese and eat it as I clear away the supper things

Figs with Raspberries and Clotted Cream

Big purple figs, as fat as they come, and deep-red raspberries, probably from Scotland at this time of year, marry beautifully with golden, crusty clotted cream.

Place the figs on a large plate, allowing two large fruits per person. Make a slit in the top of each fig and press the sides gently. It will open up like a water lily. Place a scoop of clotted cream into each fig. Scatter over the ripe raspberries – they must be really ripe – and serve.

Figs with Fraises des Bois

My local superdooper-supermarket carries *fraises des bois* early in the autumn. But don't expect to buy them at the corner shop. They twinkle like stars when scattered over a plate of open figs. Slit the figs and press them to open, then drop the little wild strawberries over the singing figs, as if you are feeding baby birds in the nest. If you judged the ripeness correctly, they will need no yoghurt, cream or honey. Just a glass of something golden and sticky.

Roast Figs

FOR 2
6 plump purple figs
butter
4 tablespoons caster sugar

Place the figs snugly in a generously buttered shallow dish. Sprinkle with a tablespoon of water and 2 tablespoons of sugar and bake in a preheated oven, 200°C/400°F (gas mark 6), for 15 minutes. Baste the figs with the syrup in the dish, then sprinkle over the remaining sugar. Bake for a further 5 minutes. Serve hot or warm, with cream or yoghurt.

Figs Baked with Honey and Lemon

FOR 2
6 fat purple figs
3 tablespoons runny honey
juice of ½ lemon

Put the figs in a shallow baking dish; they should nestle up against each other. Pour over the honey and the lemon juice. Bake for 20 minutes in a preheated oven, 200°C/400°F (gas mark 6), occasionally basting the fruit with the juices in the dish. Serve warm, perhaps with thick yoghurt.

Baked Figs with Mascarpone and Walnuts

FOR 4
12 ripe figs
50g / 2oz shelled, broken
   walnut pieces
3 tablespoons runny honey –
   a herbal one would be nice

2 tablespoons Marsala or
   medium sherry
100g / 4oz Mascarpone cheese

Cut a deep cross in the top of each fig and gently push the sides to open a hollow in each fig.

Toast the walnuts lightly under a preheated hot grill till fragrant but barely coloured. Rub off any of the skins that have come loose. There is no need to be too pernickety about this. Mix the broken nuts with the honey, alcohol and Mascarpone cheese. Fill the figs with the nut mixture.

Bake in a preheated oven, 200°C/400°F (gas mark 6), until bubbling – about 15 minutes. Serve warm.

More Figs with Mascarpone and Walnuts

Cut ripe figs in half, two or three halves per person depending on their size, and lay them on a large plate. Mix 3 tablespoons of Mascarpone cheese per person with enough double cream to make it spoonable but still voluptuous. Place a spoonful of the softened Mascarpone on to each fig half, then scatter with chopped toasted walnuts. Drizzle over a little herb honey – thyme or lavender would be more than suitable – and serve outdoors, in the autumn sunshine.

A Plate of Purple Autumn Fruits

A neighbour of mine has a fig tree. The fruit never seems to come to anything and come September the tree drops its tiny unripe fruit all over the pavement. I have forgotten how many times I have slipped on the things coming home with bags of shopping. But the leaves are a great asset. Apart from using them as cheese plates for little ash-covered goat's cheeses and other photographic uses I have used them to great effect under fruit.

Pears look wonderful on a plate of fig leaves and so, not surprisingly, do figs. A favourite plate of mine to offer after dinner is one that includes dark purple figs scattered with the last of the blackberries and a handful of pastel-coloured sugared almonds. This particular plate to be eaten before, rather than with, coffee.

DRIED FIGS

My favourite of all the dried fruits. The best, by which I mean the softest textured and the most intensely flavoured, come from Turkey. Expect the autumn harvest to be here at the end of November and to remain in good condition until early spring. The ones sold loose from cartons at the greengrocers and continental grocers' shops are invariably better than the squashed lumps in plastic bags from the health food store. Only the former are suitable to eat as dessert or as a sweet snack.

Figs and Fennel Seeds

Allow about four plump dried figs per person. Eat one first and if it has a hard stalk tucked inside it then you will have to remove them all, one by one. But it is not difficult or particularly time-consuming. Scissors or a small sharp knife will do the job best.

Split each fig in half horizontally and lay them flat on a plate. Scatter with fennel seeds and toasted flaked almonds and serve with coffee and Calvados.

A Word About Tinned Figs

Along with chickpeas and sardines, figs emerge from a can little the worse for their trauma. If you serve them very, very cold they can be really quite good. Just try not to think of fresh figs when you eat them.

Figs with Pernod

Tip a little Pernod, or Ricard, into the sticky syrup while the figs are being served. You will need no more than a few drops. A little Pernod goes a long way.

Figues Flambées

Or flaming figs. Drain the figs of their syrup. (This is not the infamous syrup of figs.) Tip the fruit into a hot frying pan, let it sizzle for a couple of minutes, then pour over a small glass of liqueur (a liqueur glass if you have such a thing). Use whichever liqueur takes your fancy, or more likely whichever bottle is open. Try a mixture of Grand Marnier and brandy, or perhaps Kirsch (make it a good one, poor Kirsch tastes like lighter fuel to me). You will need a small glass for every two figs.

Strike a light, then set fire to the pan. But not the kitchen. Turn the figs over with a fork to impregnate the fruit with the booze. But do not burn yourself. Douse the flames with a little single cream, allow to bubble once or twice and serve.

THE CRUMBLE *see also page 84–5*

If we are going to be strict about timing then the crumble doesn't really belong in this book. But the method is so absurdly simple and the pudding needs so little attention while cooking that I include it without apology.

In its simplest form it contains flour, butter, fruit and sugar, the chemistry of which magically produces comfort food of the first order. Popular additions, such as almonds or oats to the crumble topping or alcohol or extra sugar to the fruit, are I think acceptable where they do not confuse the issue. Ground almonds, just a few rubbed in with the butter and flour, are a fine idea, though I think wholemeal flour and dark brown sugar such as Muscovado ruin the flavour of both fruit and crumble.

It was Fay Maschler, restaurant critic of London's *Evening Standard*, who said, in a review of one grand old hotel's restaurant, that the 'apple crumble lacked the moment when the juices surge up and caramelise the crumbs'. Here, I think, she identified the precise point at which this homely dish becomes a success. It is not always easy to achieve, but is quite crucial.

Plums or greengages produce the finest crumbles for me. The extra juice they carry seems to do the trick, and their season is short enough not to allow me to tire of them. Rhubarb is another favourite. Damson is absolute bliss. I will admit to rating few gastronomic pleasures higher than finding a bowl of cold crumble in the fridge. And also to thinking the soggy bit between the fruit and the crisp topping the best bit of all.

Plum Crumble

If the plums you have are not as ripe as they could be but plum crumble it must be, then stew the fruit until tender for 5 minutes or so with a couple of tablespoons of sugar and water before hiding them and the juice they exude under the crumble. I have never found this necessary with really ripe fruit. The point of sprinkling water over the crumble mix before it meets the fruit is to allow some of the crumbs to stick together, giving a texture that is pebble-like rather than powdery.

FOR 4, GENEROUSLY

900g / 2lb ripe, juicy plums
sugar, to taste (probably about
   50g / 2oz)
100g / 4oz plain flour

50g / 2oz ground almonds
100g / 4oz butter
75g / 3oz caster or light brown
   sugar

Cut the plums in half and remove the stones. Place them in a large shallow baking dish. Sprinkle over as much sugar as you like. I should have suggested you taste the plums first to ascertain their sweetness.

If you have a food processor, whizz the flour, almonds and butter for a few seconds until they resemble coarse breadcrumbs. Stir in the sugar. Sprinkle the mixture with a tablespoon of cold water, and stir very lightly with a fork. Some of the crumbs should stick together but be careful not to overmix. No food processor? Then rub the butter into the flour and almonds with your fingertips, then stir in the sugar. This will take a good 5 minutes.

Scatter the crumble over the fruit and bake in a preheated oven, 200°C/400°F (gas mark 6), for about 35 minutes, until the top is crisp and golden and some of the juices from the fruit have bubbled up through the crumble.

Apricot Amaretti Crumble

FOR 4

900g / 2lb ripe apricots	100g / 4 oz plain flour
a little sugar	75g / 3oz butter
8 *amaretti* biscuits	50g / 2oz caster sugar

Pull the apricots apart and remove the stones. Place the fruit in a shallow baking dish and sprinkle over as much sugar as you would like – I suggest about 2 or 3 tablespoons – and 2 tablespoons of water.

Crush the biscuits, not too finely, in their wrappers or in a paper bag with a rolling pin. Remember, if you buy them like this, there are two biscuits in each tissue wrapping. Mix with the flour, then whizz in a food processor for a few seconds with the butter. Stir in the second lot of sugar. Sprinkle a tablespoon of water over the mixture (see recipe page 57), then mix lightly with a fork.

Tip the mixture over the apricots, then bake in a preheated oven, 200°C/400°F (gas mark 6), till golden, about 30 minutes.

* Accompany with almond cream, which is crushed *amaretti* biscuits folded into softly whipped cream

Blackberry and Apple Crumble

A classic. The apples are precooked for 5 minutes or so to give a fluffy texture that I appreciate in a pudding of this sort.

450g / 1lb tart apples, such as Bramley	100g / 4oz plain flour
	175g / 6oz butter
a little sugar	50g / 2oz rolled oats
450g / 1lb blackberries	100g / 4oz demerara sugar

Wipe the apples and cut them into quarters, then remove the cores and slice each piece in two. Put them in a pan, taste a slice for sweetness, and add a sprinkling of sugar accordingly. (I don't think even Bramleys are as tart as they should be, so you may not need much.) Add a tablespoon of water and cook over a medium heat for about 5 minutes, until the apples start to soften. Throw in the blackberries and transfer to a shallow pie dish.

Whizz the flour and butter in the food processor for a few seconds till the mixture looks like crumbs. Stir in the oats and the brown sugar and scatter over the cooked apples and blackberries. Bake in a preheated oven, 200°C/400°F (gas mark 6), for 30 minutes, or until crisp on top. Serve with double cream.

Gooseberry Crumble

Gooseberries are perfect crumble fruit, baking down to a wonderfully fragrant, soft green slush underneath the crisp, buttery topping. I am not sure that they benefit from any addition, either to topping or fruit. The simplest crumble, made from flour, butter and sugar, is more suitable here than one with oatmeal, almonds or whatever. A fine English pudding to be eaten with cold, thick, golden cream.

FOR 4

700g / 1½lb gooseberries	175g / 6oz butter
sugar	100g / 4oz caster sugar
175g / 6oz plain flour	

Pull off the worst of the stalks and the largest of the dried flowers from the gooseberries. It shouldn't take long. Place them in a shallow dish (I use a 25cm / 10 inch gratin dish) and toss gently with plenty of sugar. The amount you need depends on the tartness of the gooseberries, but they will probably need about 75g / 3oz.

Whizz the flour and butter in the food processor until it looks like coarse breadcrumbs, a matter of seconds. Stir in the second lot of sugar, sprinkle over a little water and shake the mixture or mix it gently with a fork till it resembles small pebbles. Tip the crumble on top of the fruit. Bake in a preheated oven, 200°C/400°F (gas mark 6), for 30 minutes, turning the heat up to 220°C/425°F (gas mark 7), until the top is golden and the gooseberry juices hopefully bubble up through the crumble.

Crumble Embellishments

Although I like a straightforward flour-butter-sugar topping for gooseberries and rhubarb, I happily make additions to the basic mix if I think it will improve the dish.

Ground Almonds
Substitute them for some of the flour, using a quarter to a third of the weight of the flour. Best with stone fruits such as plums and greengages.

Amaretti *Biscuits*
Continuing the almond theme, crush them to a coarse powder and either add to the flour or sprinkle on top of the finished pudding before baking. Very flattering to peaches and apricots.

Walnuts
Add just a handful of walnuts to the flour and butter as you whizz it, or crush them not too finely and scatter over the top. Best with apple and pear crumbles. Serve a drizzle of maple syrup with the cream.

Oats
Go easy on these as they are inclined to turn the pudding into something rather too earthy-tasting. Substitute 30 or 50g / 1 or 2oz

of the oats for flour. Avoid the temptation to use them with wholemeal flour unless you want to end up with a health-food-restaurant-cardboard pudding.

Spices
Cinnamon works beautifully with apple and pear, nutmeg too, while coriander will lift a peach or blackberry crumble. A few fennel seeds will do wonders for a fig or apple mixture, though ground cloves will jolt your beautiful dessert into a reminder of a childhood toothache remedy.

Grated Orange or Lemon Zest
This should be added to the fruit rather than the crumble while sesame seeds, chopped pistachios and almonds may be sprinkled on top. If they are starting to brown too quickly, turn the heat down a fraction and suffer a few minutes more cooking time.

Contemporary Crumbles

* The mincemeat one on page 84

* Blueberry, best made in half quantities unless you grow your own or are very rich. Add a mint leaf or two to the fruit and don't precook them

* Peach and Almond, use those small peaches sold in packs of twelve that invariably fail to ripen. Put almonds in the crumble and a few flaked ones on top

* Damson and Gin, scatter classic crumble topping over the compote on page 23–4, saving some of the juice for pouring over at the table

* Cherry and Almond, use fresh cherries, don't stone them unless you have time to kill, and toss the fruit with a little butter and sugar first. Use the almond crumble topping in the apricot recipe on page 58

* Dried Fruit Salad, yesterday's dried fruit salad, with some of its juices and a spoonful of brandy, has worked well on several occasions in this house

CHEESES FOR AUTUMN

I eat cheese every day in some form or another. Sometimes a lump or a slice of something with bread for lunch, or perhaps thinly sliced on toast and grilled till bubbling. More often than not cheese is eaten in my house either to end a meal or after the main course and before pudding.

I have a deep hatred of the 'cheeseboard'. A selection of four or five cheeses, usually a hard one, a soft one, a blue one and so on. Rarely are they all in fine condition, or is there ever enough of each. And you are always left with horrid bits at the end that are fit only for grating. No, give me just one cheese, a decent piece please, in perfect condition.

Cheeses do have seasons, something that you would never guess by looking at the cellophane-wrapped block cheeses in the super-markets. But proper farmhouse cheeses do have a prime time for eating. Generally speaking, and I admit it *is* a bit of a generalisation, hard cheeses are at their best when there is an 'r' in the month and soft cheeses, especially those made from goat's milk, are best in summer and autumn.

To my mind, autumn is *the* cheese season. Mushroomy, bloomy Brie de Meaux, its flavour and texture anything from mild and chalky (a pleasant enough mouthful with a Bath Oliver biscuit) to the dis-tinctly farmyardy and virtually molten. A whiff of ammonia is not a good sign. Go for a wedge cut from a whole cheese, soft and plump with a downy white rind speckled with brown, rather than something pre-cut and clingwrapped. Made at the farm and unpasteurised, it is likely to have more flavour than the creamery-made, white-rinded pasteurised versions. Camemberts, too, can be extraordinarily good at this time of year – look out for the legend *fermier* on the box; it will be a more expensive cheese but will reward you with a deeper longer-lasting flavour and a bulging, buttery texture.

Crottin de Chavignon, the diminutive goat's milk cheeses with wrinkled white rinds and chalky centres, are ripe for grilling. I have ended many a meal with one of these hard crusted little cheeses, halved horizontally and grilled till soft. There is almost a chewiness about some of them, and eaten with one of the walnut breads so popular nowadays they make a substantial and savoury alternative. Even the baby ones preserved in olive oil at the deli counter perk up with the application of a little heat.

Then there are the blues. Fourme d'Ambert, from the Auvergne, creamy, lightly piquant and reliable. Roquefort, that expensive, addictive and deeply tangy cheese, is a treat indeed. A little goes a long way. Indescribably good with sweet, dribblingly ripe pears, or with a glass of sticky Sauternes.

Lovers of pungent, creamy cheeses should seek out a Milleens. Only a decent cheese specialist will help you with this one. Made on the farm, in Ireland, from unpasteurised cow's milk, it is one of those bulging, soft, apricot-coloured cheeses with a larger-than-life smell. Grapes, slightly tart ones at that, would make an ideal partner.

Winter

2

almonds · **tropical fruits** · oranges · **fast and festive** · dates · **prunes** · cheeses

I like the first snap of winter; frosty mornings, twinkling lights and a smell of smoke in the air. Baked apple weather. For the fast foodie, there is a lot to be thankful for at this time of year. The jewel-like seeds of fat pomegranates, pastel-coloured sugared almonds, golden tropical fruits dripping with juice and citrus fruits by the bagful. Puddings don't come much faster than a glittering assortment of white iced almond paste Calisson from France scattered among nuggets of nut brittle; a plate to linger over with coffee. Or perhaps sliced Valencia oranges drizzled with Grand Marnier.

And then there's Christmas. I tend to be rather cynical about it all, but enjoy it more, rather than less, as I get older. Forgetting the crass commercialism of it, the food's the thing. The festive offerings I've given here are mostly quick ideas for the run-up to the celebrations, when you have even less time than usual. I have offered a few fast alternatives to the norm for Christmas entertaining, though you will find no 'countdown to Christmas' among these pages. I don't live the sort of life where eating can follow a timetable.

I tend to lose interest in winter after Christmas. It's only the food that keeps me going, the remnants of the chewy Turkish delight, the remains of the mincemeat and the last of the season's nuts. This is when storecupboard treats form the backbone of my dessert; any excuse not to get off the warm bus to catch the shops before they close.

Forget about picking up a punnet of something at its peak of perfection; the best puddings at this time of year have to be made from what is knocking around in the cupboards and the fruit bowl. Unlike the summer when you can upend a chip of strawberries into a bowl, puddings in the dead of winter need a little more thought.

As I have said before, improvisation is a wonderful thing.

POMEGRANATES

I don't know why most people buy pomegranates. I suspect that many of the fruits end their day sprayed gold and used as table decorations or languishing in fruit bowls for weeks on end. A pity, because ripe ones can be very good to eat. The best are as hard as tennis balls with a red blush to their creamy skin. If that skin is a little wizened then all to the good.

Those that are eaten tend to end up in fruit salads where it is almost impossible to taste their sour-sweet seeds. Far better is to serve the seeds alone, scented with flower water and sugar. Try peeling away the skin with a small knife and extracting large bite-sized nuggets with your fingers. Beware the bitter pith. Drop them into a bowl. Sprinkle over a little orange juice and a very little sugar and chill for as much time as you have. A dash of orange flower water will add a magical eastern fragrance to the fruit.

ALMONDS see also pages 19–20, 116, 133, 153

I like almonds enough to eat handful after handful of freshly shelled and roasted ones. But I find them the very devil to crack. They hardly fit into a book of fast food if it takes ten minutes to break into each nut. The ready-shelled ones in packets never taste truly fresh to me though they can be given the kiss of life by warming under the grill till fragrant.

A Plate of Almond Sweetmeats

What I really like about almonds is the confections made from them, particularly when eaten with coffee after a meal. Crisp little *amaretti* biscuits and *Calisson*, the iced almond paste sweetmeats from Provence, make a lovely end to a winter meal, especially when they share a small platter with lumps of glistening glacé fruits sparkling in the candelight.

Calisson are the most enchanting, and most fearfully expensive, of petits fours. They are made from ground almonds, crystallised orange and melon peel and coated with a thin white icing. They are usually presented in their diamond-shaped white box. Although traditionally used at Easter religious ceremonies in Aix-en-Provence, I think of them as dainty, snowy morsels to nibble after the simplest of suppers.

Amaretti, the crunchy macaroons wrapped in pastel tissue paper and sold in pillar-box-red tins, would happily share a dish with the above, but can also be put to good use to give delicate flavour and texture to creams and trifles. Each little parcel contains two semi-spherical crisp biscuits flavoured with almonds and covered in white crystals of sugar. They are particularly happy dipped into a glass of sweet wine. You could, of course, serve Amaretto di Saronno liqueur, but that might be taking the theme a little too far.

It is a tradition in our house, and I agree it is a silly one, to roll the empty *amaretti* wrappings into cylinders, stand them on their ends and set fire to them. They burn gently for a couple of seconds then rise gracefully into the air while still flaming. Of course, I am not suggesting that anything so trivial would amuse you, nor am I encouraging you to embark on ridiculous parlour games that may end in tears.

Croccante, *Turrón* and *Praline* are the Italian, Spanish and French names for the hard, sweet confection we know as nut brittle. Bought is rarely as good as home-made unless you have access to a smart food emporium that imports the stuff direct. The thinner the better. As it keeps well I tend to stock up on it, and store it in its tin. It makes a wonderfully nutty nibble with coffee.

TROPICAL FRUITS

Huge golden fruits from the tropics are at their peak during the winter months. Flown in from everywhere from Brazil to the West Indies, ripe, deeply fragrant mangoes, papayas and passion fruit have luscious, slippery flesh with intense flavours perfect for brightening up dull grey winter days.

Passion fruit   *see also page 149*
A couple of passion fruit, cut in half, make an instant finish to a meal. Inhale deeply as you eat the seeds with their scented orange-pink jelly and juice. There are few fruits quite so exquisitely scented. Heavy, wrinkly fruits provide the best eating, smooth fruits are likely to be underripe, while those light in weight will contain little joy.

There are few more effective ways of perking up a bowl of lacklustre out-of-season strawberries than a squeeze from half a passion fruit. A thickly sliced banana smothered with passion fruit seeds and juice is one of the two most enjoyable ways to start the day. For a mid-morning pick-me-up simply cut the fruit in half and suck. Those who insist on sieving out the seeds through a tea-strainer balanced over a cup are rather missing the point.

Papaya
Yellow, pear-shaped papaya shine brightest when served without adornment. Sniff rather than squeeze to check for ripeness; a highly perfumed fruit will probably be ready to eat. Cut in half from stem to navel and remove the lead-shot-like seeds with your finger, gently pulling away the fine cord that attaches them to the flesh, losing as little juice as you can. Really fine specimens will have sunset orange-pink flesh, almost jelly-like in texture. Eat with a teaspoon. The seeds, incidentally, are an extremely successful laxative.

A Plate of Golden Fruits

A large plate of delectable, ripe golden fruits from the tropics will lift the spirits like nothing else. Serve peeled papaya and mango, with pineapple if you wish, in large chunks. The fruits must be properly ripe if the dish is to be a success. Leave it in the middle of the table, embellished only by the juices you have managed to save from the fruit. Arm everyone with long, thin wooden skewers and let them help themselves. They will make a mess, of course.

Mangoes

A truly ripe mango is almost absurdly juicy. Sticky juice it is too. The most difficult part about eating a mango is not just the removal of the awkward, flat stone, but saving the precious juices that are altogether too good to waste.

Choosing a ripe mango is not always easy. Going by colour is no good at all; sometimes the rich yellow and red ones are rock hard while a green and orange fruit may be just right. Go by smell. You can often smell a truly ripe fruit from six inches. It may be even more helpful to the prospective purchaser to see a little stickiness at one end. A slight wrinkling too is a clue that tells you it is time to eat.

To serve the mango for dessert you will need to halve it. Easy enough, though I recommend you read the relevant chapter in *Jane Grigson's Fruit Book* first. At any rate you will find the mango easier to peel after cutting it in half. A peeled mango is rather like a huge, wet, dribbling bar of soap.

Hold it flat in the palm of your hand over a large bowl to catch the golden juices. Stick a small, sharp knife into the side of the fruit and work it down from one end to the other trying, as best you can, to follow the long, flat stone. You will have two shallow halves. One will contain the stone. One will inevitably be larger than the other. Cut round the stone as best you can, then remove the skin.

You could, of course, just peel it and suck the flesh from the stone. But I would rather not watch you.

Mangoes in Moscato

I have mentioned Moscato, the Italian muscat wine, before. Slices of mango marinated even for the shortest time make a tantalising dessert. Pour the wine, cold from the fridge, over the sliced fruit. One large mango and 300ml / ½ pint of wine will be enough for four.

Mango Fool

Mangoes contain something of a bargain for the quick cook in that they are rather good when used as a base for a simple pudding. Their slippery flesh marries well with cream and yoghurt, making them eligible for a smooth and delicate fool.

FOR 4
2 medium, very ripe mangoes
juice of 1 lime
150ml / ¼ pint double cream
150g / 5oz thick Greek-style yoghurt or *fromage frais*

Peel the fruit and cut it into large chunks, then liquidise it with the lime in a blender or food processor. Whip the cream until it starts to thicken, but stop well before it stands in peaks. Gently but thoroughly stir the cream and the mango purée into the yoghurt or *fromage frais*. Spoon into wineglasses and chill, if you can for 1 hour, though 20 minutes may well prove long enough.

A Tropical Fruit Salad

Cut nothing too small. The pieces of fruit should be in chunks large enough that no more than three pieces can be comfortably eaten in one spoonful.

8 lychees	2 bananas, slightly underripe
2 small, perfectly ripe mangoes	1 large papaya
¼ large ripe pineapple, or 1 baby one	4 passion fruit

Check that the fruits are ripe. If not really sweet and juicy, the salad will lose all point. The bananas will be better if slightly firm, as ripe ones turn all too easily to mush when mixed in a salad. Shell the lychees and put them in a plain china or glass bowl. Carefully peel all other fruits, apart from the passion fruit, so as not to let their juices escape. Cut the fruit into chunks, trying hard to avoid little bits, which spoil the texture of the dish. Place the fruits with their juices in the bowl.

Cut the passion fruit in half and squeeze them over the salad. Mix the fruits very gently so as not to break the pieces up. Chill for 15 minutes or so, topped with a plate to keep other flavours out and the wonderful fruit fragrance in.

WINTER ORIENTALS

Persimmons
Persimmons have a texture quite unlike that of any other fruit. When ready to eat they resemble tender, swollen, glowing globes filling to bursting with jelly-like flesh. Ripeness is all. Buy the fruit slightly underripe and finish it off in a brown paper bag. Choose a truly ripe one and you will be lucky to get it home before its delicate skin breaks and fills your shopping bag with orange slush. A persimmon is ready to eat when it looks on the point of bursting. Eat an underripe fruit and you will never forget it.

Persimmons and Cream

I remain unconvinced you can improve a persimmon by turning it into a pie. If you want to gild this particular lily then the most delicious way to do it is with cream. Thick, yellow, double cream.

Take a slice off the top of the ripe persimmon as if you are breaking into a soft-boiled egg. Serve each 'pot' with a teaspoon and a tiny pot of cream (you will need a 100ml / 4fl oz pot between four), pouring a little of the cream into the fruit each time you scoop out a spoonful of its tender flesh.

Lychees

Lychees have a rough, brown and pink shell, which is easily peeled away to reveal the transluscent white knob of flesh within. They make a dramatic display for dessert, especially if you have made the trip to Chinatown for those sold on the stem. Once inside, suck the fruit from the large brown seed or, if it is to end up in a fruit salad, split the fruit in half down one side and ease out the stone.

Physalis

Physalis is probably better known as the Cape Gooseberry. Easier to remember but hardly appropriate. The papery magic-lantern husk can be folded back to reveal a waxy-skinned, cherry-sized orange fruit. Its sweet-sour flavour is interesting enough to include it as part of a plate of assorted tropical fruit, but I am not sure I would want to eat a whole plateful.

ORANGES *see also pages 108, 149, 173*

Nothing brightens up a grey winter's day like a firm-fleshed juicy orange. The joy of the orange is fourfold: the aromatic zest, the copious juice, the refreshing flesh and the fragrant water that has been perfumed by its flowers. All four are of interest to those in a hurry for a winter dessert.

Oranges do not naturally shine. On the tree their pitted, fragrant skin has a soft dustiness, to my eye far more tempting than the vicious glare of the ones for sale in this country. But that is what we have. A few stores offer unwaxed alternatives, but these are hardly in abundance.

Unfortunately, it is the zest I want, not the wax. Neither do I relish the pesticides and fungicides that lurk under that polish. Washing is the only answer, though I am convinced that the best of the zest will be lost. To make matters worse, oranges lose much of their aromatic quality during shipping. We must make the best of what we have.

Choose fruits that are heavy for their size. And I need not remind you that size is not everything. Thin-skinned fruit is often juicier than thick, though less easy to grate for zest.

The zest is the very essence of the orange. It is the outermost skin of the fruit, and should contain none of the white pith, which is horribly bitter. A small, sharp knife or a grater will remove the zest but you will have to keep a close watch not to remove the pith.

Bananas with Orange Zest

A fine way to show off this part of the orange.

FOR 2

juice of 3 medium oranges and the zest from 1
juice of 1 lime
4 bananas, slightly underripe

Remove the zest from one of the oranges using the fine side of a grater. (Rest the zester on a plate rather than a chopping board. The orange zest will take up past flavours from your board like a sponge and will then add them to your dessert.) Scrape the zest into a white bowl.

Squeeze the juice from the oranges and the lime and add to the zest. Skin the banana and slice into rounds almost 1cm / ½ inch thick.

Macerate them in the juice and zest for 15 minutes, but no longer lest they become fuzzy and soft.

Sunday Oranges

I often find that on grey winter Sunday afternoons there is little that goes down better than a huge platter of peeled and sliced oranges and baby citrus fruits placed in the centre of the table. The more varieties the better. Passing round glasses of one of the orange-flavoured muscats, such as Brown Brothers', as chilled as it can be, will help make the sun shine.

A Salad of Oranges and Winter Strawberries

It seems a shame to ignore the punnets of red strawberries around in the winter, though they are rarely worth buying to eat for themselves. The orange zest and juice here will lift their spirits. The seediness of out-of-season strawberries adds a welcome crunch.

FOR 4
5 oranges
2 tablespoons orange flower water
225g / 8oz strawberries

Remove the zest from one of the oranges, making sure that you grate none of the white pith with it. Cut the orange in half and squeeze the juice from it into a bowl with the zest. Stir in the orange flower water. Cut the peel from the remaining oranges with a sharp knife, taking care to remove all the pith. Slice the oranges into rounds as thick as pound coins and place in the bowl with the zest and scented juice.

   Wipe the strawberries, remove their green leaves and cut them in half. Add them to the oranges and toss very gently. Serve lightly chilled if you can. Remember that if you are short of time an ice cube or two tossed in with the fruit will reduce the chilling time to 15 minutes or so. Keep in the fridge and remove the ice before it melts and dilutes your lovely scented juice.

Chilled Oranges

A little forethought required here. Place large, firm oranges such as Navel or Valencia in the fridge overnight. When thoroughly chilled, cut them into quarters from stalk to flower end. Eat them with your hands.

Baked Cinnamon Oranges with Grand Marnier

I find the warm deep orange notes of Grand Marnier useful for perking up fruit that proves less interesting than it looked in the shop. I include it here for its fragrance, which wafts up as you open the steamy parcel. Use Cointreau if that is what you have.

FOR 2

2 large oranges
1 tablespoon brown sugar

½ cinnamon stick or a little of
    the powdered spice
Grand Marnier

Set the oven to 200°C/400°F (gas mark 6). Tear off two squares of foil large enough to wrap up the oranges. Peel the fruit with a sharp knife, taking care to remove all the pith, and cut into slices horizontally about as thick as pound coins. Bring the slices together to re-form the oranges, put on to the foil squares and sprinkle with the sugar. Break the half cinnamon stick in half again and divide between the parcels, or dust very lightly with powdered cinnamon. Go easy with the ground variety, which lacks the subtlety of the spice when still in the stick.

Bring the edges of the foil up around each fruit to form a parcel. Add a few drops of Grand Marnier (a teaspoon each is probably about right, but you must judge that for yourself). Scrunch the foil together at the top of each orange and bake for 10–15 minutes, till warmed through and fragrant. Open at the table and inhale its pungent, fruity scent.

Two-orange Salad

I look forward to the arrival of blood oranges in the winter as much as I do raspberries in the summer. I flatly refuse to call them ruby oranges or whatever name Marks and Sparks has thought up for them. Blood oranges, if we are lucky, will last a good two months in the shops during mid-winter. Their flavour is slightly sharper than that of a Navel, and the drink is the prettiest sunset pink. A straight-forward salad, devoid of liqueurs or zest, is my way to eat them.

Peel two medium oranges and two blood oranges, taking care not to leave any white pith on the fruit. Slice the oranges about 10mm / $1/3$ inch thick. Collect all the juice you can. Lay the slices on two plates alternating the dark and light fruits. Drizzle over any of the juice you have saved. That's it.

CLEMENTINES, TANGERINES AND MANDARINS

Wooden crates of neat flat-topped little citrus fruits appear in the shops in late autumn. They are the first real signs that winter is on its way. The ones sporting occasional foil-wrapped fruits are annual reminders that Christmas is inevitable.

These small citrus fruits are the most useful of all, keeping well and taking just seconds to peel. A few little fruits lurking at the bottom of the fruit bowl can be transformed into a bright dessert within minutes. I am rarely sure which of the endless variety I have bought until I start to peel them.

Satsumas have found favour lately. More favour than flavour. I suspect this popularity is for their ease of peeling. Much more interesting are the clementines and mandarins, tighter skinned but bursting with juice and sweetness, though they stay in good condition for marginally less time. Easy-peel hybrids with names that smack of boardroom compromise, clemenvillas, jafferines and ortaniques are with us on and off throughout the season.

All are worth trying for their subtle differences of acidity and sweetness. Go for ones with their dark green, pointed leaves still attached, if you are given the choice, or go for the red net bags of twenty or so, which usually represent good value. The fruits' collective Latin name is *Citrus reticulata*, and means netted, a reference no doubt to their lacy pith rather than a far-sighted prediction of twentieth-century packaging techniques. Expect them to hang around till April.

Tangerines with Caramel Cream

FOR 2
6 juicy tangerines, clementines or some such small citrus fruit
100g / 4oz caster sugar
225ml / 8fl oz double cream

Peel the little fruits, removing as much of the pith as you have patience for. Slice them thinly and divide between two plates. Put the sugar in a small pan over a medium heat and cook till it turns golden brown, watching carefully to catch the golden brown caramel before it suddenly turns into thick, acrid smoke. Remove from the heat.

Bring the cream slowly to the boil in another small pan over a medium heat. When it boils let it reduce at a steady simmer for a minute, then pour into the caramel pan, whisking the mixture slowly. Bring the caramel cream slowly back up to heat, then pour it around the oranges.

The Christmas Pudding

Nothing sends me to sleep quite like a bowl of Christmas pudding. And with its six or seven hours' boiling time, you may be surprised to see this fruity, spicy, festive pudding in this book. Yet its fine ingredients are altogether too good to miss and can be assembled as a grand dessert to be offered instead. On the other hand, a cold Christmas pudding provides rich pickings for post-Christmas snacks.

A Christmas Plate

Take the most interesting ingredients that go into a Christmas pudding and pile them high on a huge oval platter in the centre of the table. The quality will have to be superb and the portions generous. Huge, seedy raisins still on the vine are available from the poshest shops and can be set among sticky, uncoloured glacé cherries, sugary slices of uncut orange and citron peel and fat, golden sultanas. (From Italian grocers.) Scatter whole skinned almonds and dried figs among the rest, with handfuls of clementines to represent the grated zest. You can forget the suet and the currants, but not the silver three-penny bit hidden at the bottom. Offer brandy to drink, but a better one than you would have put in the pudding.

A Couple of Things to Do with Leftover Christmas Pudding

I include the following suggestions on the assumption that well after the feasting has finished you will find some cold Christmas pudding at the back of the fridge, and will then look for a good way to use it up.

Vanilla Ice Cream with Christmas Pudding Sauce

The best Christmas puddings are fruity and alcoholic, rich and moist. Push these qualities to the limit and you end up with a fine sauce that marries happily with hard vanilla ice cream straight from the freezer.

FOR 4

175g / 6oz Christmas pudding
30g / 1oz butter
30g / 1oz brown sugar

juice of ½ orange
3 tablespoons brandy
vanilla ice cream for 4

Crumble the pudding between your fingers into a shallow pan. Set over a low heat, then add the butter and sugar. Mix in the orange juice and the brandy with a wooden spoon and bring slowly to a fierce bubble. Turn down the heat and simmer gently while you place a ball or two of ice cream in four individual bowls. Spoon over the Christmas pudding sauce and serve immediately.

Fried Christmas Pudding with Apricot Sauce

Not as rich as you might fear, though I wouldn't eat much more than a cold turkey sandwich beforehand. Use your prettiest plates for this, otherwise everyone will think you are giving them black pudding.

FOR EACH PERSON

30g / 1oz butter
2 × 75g / 3oz slices of cold
  Christmas pudding
2 tablespoons apricot jam

1 tablespoon brandy
1 tablespoon water
double cream, to serve

Melt the butter in a frying pan, put in the slices of pudding and fry till lightly crisp on each side. Transfer to a plate with a fish slice (the pudding is now very crumbly), and keep warm. Melt the jam in the same pan over a medium heat, add the brandy and the water and bring to the boil, mashing the lumps in the jam against the side of the pan till smooth enough to call a sauce. Spoon over the sauce and a drizzle of cream.

The Christmas Cake – A Few Alternatives

The traditional iced and marzipanned fruit cake has fewer devotees than the Christmas pudding. A pretty and I think altogether more tempting alternative is to arrange a plate of associated sugary confections for each guest to dip into at will. Try sugared almonds, just the white ones this time, squares of white almond paste or a few marzipan fruits (if you find some that are not luridly coloured and taste of bubblegum), and thin slices of *panforte*, that dense and chewy spice cake from Siena. Or perhaps a handful of the French nougat with the rice-paper wrapping that sticks to your lips.

At the risk of sounding tacky (and what could possibly be tackier than a Christmas cake), this plate looks wonderful when mounded high and tied up with white ribbon. At least your guests will think you care. Which, of course, you do, otherwise you would have bought a boring ready-made cake from the supermarket.

Panforte
You could present one of those huge *panforte* instead of a cake. A far better idea to my mind. The Italians make them in Siena; they fill them with all manner of dried fruits and nuts, then wrap them in paper. You can find them all year round here in Italian grocers' shops. Spiced with cinnamon and sweetened with honey, they have a delectable texture poised somewhere between fruit cake and nougat. Set a large one on the table, like a huge Brie, then cut it into slivers and serve it with Vinsanto, the sweet Italian fortified wine. You can expect even the smallest one to feed about six.

Panettone
Best of all, I think, is *panettone*, the Italian Christmas bread. Originally from Lombardy, this dome-shaped bread is both light and rich at the

same time. Scattered through with sultanas and citrus peel, its texture lies somewhere between a brioche and a light fruit loaf. If you have bought one before, initially splendid in its fez-shaped box but unexciting in reality (an overblown fairy cake is one description that springs to mind), then I implore you to take another look. Choose one from a busy grocer's shop, turn the box over – it will probably be hanging from the ceiling by its ribbon – and check the sell-by date. (*Da consumarsi preferibimente entro* is actually what you are looking for.) Eat it, in thick slices, buttered or not. It is perfect for dunking in milky coffee. Resist the temptation of the chocolate chip version, to my mind too much of a good thing altogether. Use your *panettone* in any of the following ways, some traditionally Italian and festive, others positively *nuovo*.

Pan-fried Panettone *and Mincemeat Sandwich*

A crisp, sweet and buttery snack that somehow tastes and smells like the very essence of Christmas. I eat it as a mid-morning pick-me-up with coffee, though I have often been tempted to cut the bread into elegant rounds with fluted cutters and serve it up with cream as a smart pudding. In which case I would serve it with a peeled and sliced clementine on each plate.

FOR EACH PERSON
1 slice of *panettone*, 10mm / ¹/₃ inch thick
2 tablespoons good mincemeat
30g / 1oz butter

Cut the slice of *panettone* in half. Spread one semi-circle with mincemeat. Press the other half gently on top. Melt the butter in a small frying pan; when it bubbles add the sandwich and fry till golden brown on both sides. Remove with a palette knife, cut in half and eat while hot and crisp.

Panettone Perdu

FOR 2

4 slices of *panettone*, crusts
  removed
150ml / ¼ pint milk
2 tablespoons sugar

1 small egg, beaten
butter, for frying
ground cinnamon and caster
  sugar, for dusting

Cut each round of bread into quarters. Sweeten the milk with the
sugar. Dip each piece of bread into the milk, then into the beaten
egg and fry it on both sides in a little hot butter until crisp. Expect it
to take about 3 minutes per side. Remove, drain on kitchen paper
and sprinkle with some caster sugar and a subtle dusting of cinnamon. Eat hot.

Hot Panettone *Pudding*

A rather classy bread and butter pudding.

FOR 4

4 tablespoons raisins
2 tablespoons eau de vie
75g / 3oz butter
150g / 5oz *panettone*

2 eggs
300ml / ½ pint double cream
75g / 3oz sugar

Set the oven to 180°C/350°F (gas mark 4). Scatter the raisins and the
eau de vie in a shallow dish, about 23 or 25cm / 9 or 10 inches in
diameter. Melt the butter in a shallow pan, and tear the bread into
chunks. They should be about 2.5cm / 1 inch long. Fry the *panettone*
in the butter for a couple of minutes till golden; you will need a
reasonably high heat but watch that the whole lot does not burn.
Tip it into the dish with the buttery juices. Mix the last three ingredients with a whisk, then pour over the *panettone*. Bake until risen and
golden, about 25 minutes. Serve warm.

* For a sweet snack, slice the cake into rounds, slightly thicker than

you would bread for toast, and grill till very lightly coloured. Butter it if you wish, though I am not sure it is necessary. Avoid the temptation to slot it into the toaster. The rich bread crumbles when warm and you will only end up fishing it out in bits

* Anna Del Conte, Milanese cook, translator and teacher, suggests in her inspiring book, *Entertaining All'Italiana*, her idea of warming slices in the oven for 10 minutes, then serving them with Mascarpone cheese, which 'voluptuously melts in contact with the hot *panettone*'

Mincemeat *see also page 82*

I approve of progress. Particularly the sort that involves the slow transformation of mincemeat from the boiled mutton, shredded beef suet, raisins, ginger and rosewater of the sixteenth century to the sweet, fruity and spicy preserve it is today. Although I will concede that most commercial stuff is too sweet and benefits from a dose of grated orange zest and a good slug of lemon juice.

I have already mentioned that the confection makes a good sandwich filling for sweet bread such as *panettone*, but I have also found several other quick uses for the sad little jar that has a tendency to lurk on the shelf till you throw it away next Christmas.

Christmas Crumble

I keep this pudding for those occasions when only something sweet, rich and rib-sticking in the extreme will do. It takes a bit longer than 30 minutes. (Forty actually.)

FOR 4

350g / 12oz dessert apples
450g / 1lb good mincemeat
1 large banana
juice of 1 small orange

100g / 4oz flour
75g / 3oz butter
50g / 2oz sugar

Set the oven to 200°C/400°F (gas mark 6). Slice the apples fairly thinly (it is not necessary to peel them) and put them in a 900ml / 2 pint pudding basin or similar (a 15cm / 6 inch soufflé dish, for instance), then stir in the mincemeat, the banana sliced into thick rounds and the orange juice.

Whizz the last three ingredients in a food processor (a few seconds) or work them to crumbs with your fingers (a few minutes), then drizzle over a few drops of water and stir. A few of the crumbs will stick together, which makes for a crumbly, rather than powdery texture. Bake till crisp on top, about 25–30 minutes.

* Follow the recipe for the jam omelette on page 100–101, substituting mincemeat for the jam

* Navel Oranges with Mincemeat Sauce is about the quickest thing you can do with mincemeat short of wolfing it straight from the jar. Although I have used this fruity sauce as an accompaniment to ice cream and a slice of almond spongecake, I find two or three huge slices from a large, cold, sweet orange a far better foil. Peel a large orange with a sharp knife to get rid of the peel and white pith, saving the juices as you go. The colder the orange the better. Slice it into six rounds and lay three slices on each of two plates. Add the juice from ½ lemon and a tablespoon of brandy to 100g / 4oz mincemeat. Bring to the boil in a small pan and turn down to a gentle simmer for 2 or 3 minutes. Spoon around the oranges and serve. Enough for two

DATES

There is something about dates that seems as old as time itself. I am not as keen on the fresh ones, packed in Israel, as some. They have tough skins and a fibrous, almost whiskery, texture, which does not appeal to me. Some of the dry-skinned, lightly wrinkled Medjool variety, sold in plastic trays in chain stores and in loose boxes in

Middle Eastern grocers, are very fine indeed. They belong on a dessert plate with squares of dark, but not bitter chocolate, and some slices of crystallised orange peel.

Good though these are, I would miss the ubiquitous oblong packs of semi-dried dates, the ones with the useless sticky prong and the paper doiley that always sticks to the last few dates. I have a soft spot for their sweet stickiness. They are usually the Deglet Noor variety, a plump date less wrinkled than some. Everyone seems to agree that these dates have an affinity with dairy produce. Yoghurt, cold and thick, works well as a dip for stoned dates, while a small knob of butter concealed in the hollow left by the stone is popular with many.

I recently read Jane Grigson's chapter on dates in her wonderful *Fruit Book*. Having eaten dates all my life, spitting out the stones cherry-style, I was horrified to read that it is unwise to do so as many of the fibres round the stones contain little insects. The first two dates I checked were distinctly dodgy. There are some things it is better not to know.

Hot Buttered Dates

A sticky, buttery plateful this, showing the dates' natural sweetness to the full. A drizzle of yoghurt, a sharp one if possible, will cut through the dish's sweetness like a knife. Six dates each is quite enough.

FOR 2

30g / 1oz butter

12 fresh or dried dates

1 tablespoon flaked almonds

juice of ½ small orange

Melt the butter in a shallow pan. When it sizzles add the dates. Cook over a medium heat, taking care that the dates and butter do not burn by constantly shaking the pan. When the dates have plumped up slightly, toss in the almonds, allowing them to brown slightly, then deglaze the pan with the orange juice, scraping up any sugary sediment there might be. Bubble the liquid for 30 seconds or so to reduce it slightly, then spoon the mixture on to warm plates. Serve drizzled with yoghurt.

* Split open a handful of Medjool dates and pull out the stones. Mix a little freshly grated orange zest into a lump of almond paste with your fingers. Break off small lumps and stuff each date with it

* Dip Medjool dates in melted chocolate, then leave to harden

* Add chopped, stoned dates (not the rock-hard blocks of stoned dates) to your breakfast yoghurt. Stir in a handful of rolled oats and some roughly chopped almonds

Date, Almond and Honey Cakes

Hot, crunchy, sticky little date cakes. The crunchy nuts are an important element, so don't overprocess the mixture. Likewise, overcooking will result in dryness. Boxed, moist dates are inclined to work better here than the drier ready-pitted ones packed in cellophane.

FOR 4

150g / 5oz dried dates, stones removed
100g / 4oz unskinned almonds
75g / 3oz melted butter
90g / 3½oz plain flour

1 tablespoon runny honey, such as orange blossom
thick, Greek-style yoghurt and more honey, to serve

Squeeze the stones from the dates. This will give you about 100g / 4oz of sticky pulp. Whizz them with the almonds in the food processor for a few seconds to give a coarse mixture, then pour in half the melted butter. Add the flour and the honey and whizz briefly to mix thoroughly. Don't overprocess at this stage, which will result in the little cakes losing their texture.

Scoop out small handfuls of mixture and squash into patties about

5cm / 2 inches in diameter; you will probably get about ten or a dozen. Heat the remaining butter in a shallow pan and fry the patties for about 3 minutes on each side, till golden brown, turning them once. Eat while hot, on warm plates, with a dollop of yoghurt and a drizzle of honey.

Date and Bacon Savoury

Remove the stones from fresh or dried dates, then roll up each one in a streaky rasher of bacon. Secure with a cocktail stick, then grill till the bacon fat is golden and the meat is bordering on the crisp. Allow four per person. Eat hot.

PRUNES *see also pages 104, 116*

Prunes make people laugh. Even those who dislike them. I love the things, but rarely resist some schoolboy-style joke while offering them around, even though I have never found their dark reputation to be particularly deserved.

The best prunes I have ever eaten are the vacuum-packed ones labelled *pruneaux d'Agen*. Moist and deeply flavoured, they are succulent enough to eat straight from the bag. These are the ones I would choose to offer for dessert, though the slightly drier Californian ones are fine general-purpose fruits, often grown from the same stock.

A Prune Plate

A handful of prunes, the plumpest and moistest you can find, can be offered on a large plate as dessert. Set them with complementary flavours such as squares of chocolate (though nothing too dark and bitter on this occasion) and cubes of almond paste. A scattering of shelled and toasted whole almonds works well here too.

Prunes with Vanilla Ice Cream and an Aromatic Syrup

FOR 2

150g / 5oz *pruneaux d'Agen*
250ml / 9fl oz red wine
½ teaspoon fennel seeds
1 small orange, sliced

2 tablespoons runny honey
a small sprig of thyme
2 bay leaves

Put everything in a small, heavy-based pan with 2 tablespoons of water. Bring to the boil, turn down the heat and simmer very gently for 25 minutes. Check from time to time that the liquid isn't boiling away.

Remove the fruit to a warm bowl with a draining spoon. Turn up the heat under the liquid. Watching it carefully, let it boil until it becomes a rich syrup. It will probably take barely 2 minutes. Taste it using a cold spoon. You may think it needs more honey, but it isn't really meant to be very sweet. Pour the syrup over the prunes.

Serve in deep-rimmed plates or bowls, a ball of white vanilla ice cream in the centre, the prunes and aromatics hugging it closely, with the deep, claret-coloured syrup spooned over them. Eat immediately.

CHEESES FOR WINTER

However loudly I sing the praises of British cheeses there is nothing that comes within shouting distance of a truly ripe Vacherin. For me it is the perfect example of the cheesemaker's art. Cosy in its bark casket, the pinky-orange, bloomy rind hides a creamy, mild, molten inside that tastes of butter and grass and smells like old gym shoes. Press the rind gently, it will feel alive, as if there is something voluptuous lurking within. Which there is. Serve the cheese by cutting a slice, cake-like, and scooping out the liquid contents as best you can with a spoon.

Stilton, yes, but there are better blues for Christmas eating. A

Cashel Blue, bulging with ripeness, will offer more in terms of flavour and interest though will be less reliable. Cashel Blue has been made in Ireland, from unpasteurised milk, for the last two decades. Its mottled, browny-red rind does all it can to contain the soft, blue-veined, creamy interior. Bloated, oozing specimens are not necessarily over the top; in fact, they are probably at their peak. Though some may prefer their cheese younger and firmer, when the flavour will be mildly piquant. An after-dinner cheese of the finest order.

Not that there is anything wrong with Stilton, I am just a little tired of being offered cling-wrapped, wet, sweaty portions instead of the real thing. There are plenty of bad examples about, so check carefully that it is creamy-textured rather than wet, that it has no yellowing, cracked edges and it smells faintly musty rather than of sweaty socks. Ask to taste it. It should be creamy yellow, with enough blue-grey veining to make it interesting. The flavour should be neither too strong nor too salty. If you like it, buy it. And buy enough. It makes wonderful, smelly, bubbling, cheese on toast.

Spring 3

eggs and batters · **bananas** · creams and
cream cheeses · **staples and stodge** ·
chocolate · **cheeses**

*S*pring is two seasons really, bridging the months from
steamed puddings to ice cream. This is the season that spans
the gap between the first crocuses in the snow and the first
attempts at eating out of doors.

The spring chapter is a collection of ideas which, although
seasonal, would also fit into the winter and summer pages too.
I am not suggesting you confine your love of chocolate to Easter
or the making of pancakes to Shrove Tuesday, but as subjects
they do seem to sit more comfortably in this chapter than any
of the others. At least that's my excuse. That is why this section
runs the gamut from comforting clafoutis to lacy pancakes, and
hot chocolate soufflé to espresso ice cream.

Here you will find everything from batter puddings, chocolate
sauces and creamy rice puddings to creams, ices and sorbets.
Early spring has little to offer the fruit lover, but sweet pineapples
and bananas are at their peak from March to May. Other more

interesting fruits have yet to appear in good enough condition at affordable prices.

This is the time of year I get closest to baking. A sweet version of Yorkshire pudding with pears rolled in brandy is about as near as it gets. I have a little more time, though not much, at this time of year and might get as far as making crêpes and even little soufflés. That said, I don't want to spend more than an hour cooking, and still refuse to spend much more than half of that on the dessert.

EGGS AND BATTERS

Rustic batter puddings, featherweight crêpes and nursery-pudding-style custards exploit the versatile egg to the full. What more delicious way to end a meal is there than a crisp-topped clafoutis with its cargo of cherries and irresistibly soggy centre? It is not the fastest of puds, and many a purist would banish it from this book, but so easy is its making and so basic its ingredients that I really cannot miss it out.

If you only make crêpes once a year, then I urge you to try them for a quick pudding after a light lunch. You can whizz the batter in the blender in seconds, and you don't have to leave it to rest. But having access to a pan that does not stick is pretty much essential.

Custards too can be fast food. A proper custard, creamy and scented with vanilla, takes little more than 10 or 15 minutes to make. Easily accomplished while you are doing something else at the stove anyway, such as cooking pasta. Throw in a few sliced bananas and you have one of the all-time-great British puddings.

Custard

I am not shy of taking short cuts. But custard powder is not one of them. I find it deeply cloying, smothering the flavour of anything it is served with, and I would rather serve cream or yoghurt than packet custard. No, if it is to be custard then real custard it must be.

It doesn't take long. Just bring the milk and cream to the boil, pour it over the egg yolks and sugar and return to a clean pan, stirring over a low heat till cooked. It rarely takes longer than 10 minutes, though I have known it take 15. It is not difficult if you remember:

* It needs a little concentration

* To rinse out the pan before you return the custard to it

* That custard is not really meant to be as thick as the packet stuff and, most importantly, that all will end in disaster if you let it become too hot

If you have stuck to the instructions like glue and the result of your efforts still shows signs of curdling, then zap it into the blender with a little more milk or cream and whizz for a few seconds. It will still be a bit grainy but no one will notice.

Classic Custard

You can add a drop of vanilla extract at the end if you haven't any vanilla pods.

FOR 1

300ml / ½ pint mixed milk and cream

1 vanilla pod

1 large egg plus 1 egg yolk

3 tablespoons caster sugar

Put the milk and cream into a heavy-based saucepan set over a medium heat. Cut the vanilla pod lengthways and drop it into the pan. Bring to boiling point; the milk will be quivering and a few bubbles will rise when it is ready. (Watch it closely, as the milk takes just seconds to swoosh up the pan and cascade over the cooker.)

While the milk is coming to the boil beat the egg and egg yolk with the sugar in a heatproof bowl. The mixture should be pale and creamy. The milk is probably ready now. Put a sieve over the egg and sugar and pour in a little of the warm milk, remove the sieve and stir well. Add the rest of the milk through the sieve, then rinse out the saucepan so that no bits remain on the bottom. Pour in the custard and return the pan to the heat. At this point, I always scrape the black seeds from the vanilla pod with the point of a knife and stir them into the custard.

Cook over a gentle flame, stirring slowly and continuously, for a good 5 or 6 minutes, until the custard has thickened slightly. Pour into a jug.

* At the first sign of curdling or graininess, remove the bowl from the heat. Place in a sink of cold water and whisk energetically till smooth.

Yoghurt Custard

When even 15 minutes is beyond me, or when I want something that is lighter and sharper (that is, for fruits or for spooning over chocolate cake), I make a yoghurt version.

The joy of this custard is that its slight piquancy lifts whatever it accompanies rather than suffocating it. It is virtually foolproof – I can make it – and it takes considerably less time than the traditional hot milk and cream variety. It is not my recipe at all; the idea has been borrowed from a friend, the gardener-cook Lynda Brown.

Lynda Brown's Yoghurt Custard

FOR EACH PERSON
1 large egg yolk
75–100ml / 3–4fl oz plain yoghurt (Lynda uses home-made)
a generous teaspoon or slightly more runny honey

Put all the ingredients in a small pan over a gentle heat and keep stirring until the mixture comes to the boil and has thickened.

Flower Blossom Yoghurt Custard

Make the yoghurt custard above, adding flower water, either orange or rose, as soon as it has thickened. About 2 teaspoons of fine quality will do, though you may like a little more. Serve warm, in small wineglasses, with nutty biscuits.

Banana Custard

You might have guessed I would hold the same affection for banana custard that I do for mashed potatoes (see *Real Fast Food*).

Follow either of the custard recipes. Pour the result into a warmed bowl (run under the hot tap if necessary), then add the sliced fruit.

The banana needs to be pretty ripe, so choose a well-freckled one, and slice it thinly, though in pieces no thinner than one pound coins. Leave the slices in the custard for a good 5 minutes before eating; it takes a while for the flavour to impregnate the sauce.

Reckon on one banana per person, the above recipe making enough for two.

Zabaglione

I used to be terrified of this stuff. I usually am of anything I am not too sure how to pronounce. *Zabaglione*, *Zabaione* or, in French, *Sabayon* is the magical transformation of eggs, sugar and wine, via heat and elbow grease, into a thick frothy voluptuous custard. It is probably as old as the hills and, despite its name, is absurdly easy.

The work involved is simply that of beating the mixture while it warms in a bowl over hot water. A hand-held electric whisk will save you getting beater's cramp (there is little less appetising than watching someone break into a sweat when they are cooking). Some people avoid making this because it demands last-minute attention, which is why it is suitable for those whose entertaining is of the casual kind. Like hot fritters, it is ideal for informal meals where you are eating in the kitchen, then at least your guests might offer to hold the whisk for a while. Expect it to take 12–15 minutes. Which is why you need an electric whisk.

Just one word of caution, though: do not allow the bottom of the bowl to touch the hot water in the pan, or the water to do more than simmer. If the mixture overheats you will have something extremely unappealing in your bowl.

I like easily remembered formulae. They got me through my exams. Except the accountancy ones – which I failed spectacularly. Recipes are no exception, and I make this version of *zabaglione* rather than any other because I can remember it without looking it up. It is also a really good one.

FOR 6
4 egg yolks
100g / 4oz caster sugar
100ml / 4fl oz Marsala

Beat the egg yolks with the sugar in a bowl with an electric whisk. Add the Marsala and place the bowl over a pan of simmering water. Do not let the bowl touch the water or you will have scrambled eggs. Do not answer the phone, or pour yourself a drink unless it is from the Marsala bottle, and do not try to clear away the main course dishes. Just beat.

When the mixture is thick and frothy – it should virtually stand in peaks – it is ready. Ladle the *zabaglione* into glasses and serve immediately while it is still warm and sensual.

A Few Good Things to Stir, Sprinkle or Dunk into a Classic *Zabaglione*

* Vanilla: use pure vanilla extract and beat it in after all the other ingredients have started to thicken

* Cinnamon: either add a little ground spice to the mixture as it is thickening, or sprinkle some over the top

* Chocolate: just as the mixture finishes thickening, stir in a handful of chocolate, shaved, with the help of a vegetable peeler, from a dark and bitter block

* Italian *biscotti*, especially the hard ones with almonds embedded in them, are the best for *zabaglione*-dunking. Rich Tea fingers aren't bad either

* Whipped cream: fold in softly whipped cream (you will need 100ml / 4fl oz of double cream to 4 egg yolks) to give a rich, thick pudding suitable for serving cold, or just tepid if you cannot wait

Banana Zabaglione

This is another version of my favourite pudding, bananas and custard.

FOR 6

the egg yolk, sugar and sweet wine quantities opposite, plus 2 ripe bananas

Make the *zabaglione* as on page 97. While it is still warm stir in the bananas, sliced as thinly as pound coins. Serve in glasses and eat while still warm.

Strawberry Zabaglione

To the classic recipe above add a handful or two of sliced ripe strawberries. A nice almondy biscuit would go down well too, I expect.

Zabaglione *with Blackcurrant Purée*

FOR 6

225g / 8oz frozen blackcurrants
1 tablespoon sugar
4 egg yolks

100g / 4oz caster sugar
100ml / 4fl oz Marsala or other
sweet white wine

Put the blackcurrants in a pan with the 1 tablespoon of sugar and a tablespoon of water. Cook over a medium heat till the fruit burst and a thick purple syrup forms, about 5 or 6 minutes.

Put the yolks, second lot of sugar and sweet wine in a bowl over a pan of simmering water and beat till thick with an electric whisk. Expect this to take about 10–15 minutes. Switch off the heat.

Spoon 2 tablespoons of the fruit and its juice into six glasses, top up with spoonfuls of *zabaglione* and eat with a teaspoon, marbling the rich purple juice and golden custard as you eat.

The Twenty-minute Tiramisu

Tiramisu is that creamy, alcoholic mess of sponge cake and cream cheese. A sort of Italian trifle. No longer hip, it is rarely seen on menus outside the occasional wine bar. Addicts must therefore make it themselves. Traditionally, it is made the night before so that the sponge will soak up the liquid and the cream cheese topping thickens somewhat. I will not argue with the importance of this, but, for addicts such as myself, this quick version is not so very far away from the real thing.

FOR 4 (OR 2 ADDICTS)

20 sponge fingers from a packet
175ml / 6fl oz very strong coffee,
   preferably espresso
7 tablespoons Marsala or, if you
   must, sweet sherry
4 eggs

4 tablespoons sugar
450g / 1lb Mascarpone cheese
30g / 1oz bitter chocolate,
   grated or 2 tablespoons cocoa
   powder

Break up the sponge fingers into short lengths and drop them into a shallow serving dish, then mix the coffee and the Marsala and pour it over the biscuits. Press them down into the liquid; they must soak it all up.

Separate the eggs: yolks in one large bowl, whites in another. Beat the egg yolks and the sugar with an electric whisk, then mix in the Mascarpone. Rinse the beaters, then whisk the egg whites till stiff. Scoop them into the Mascarpone and mix thoroughly with a metal spoon. Spoon the Mascarpone mixture over the softened sponge cakes. Spread reasonably flat, then grate over the chocolate or dust with cocoa powder.

Leave for as long as you can before serving; even 10 minutes in the fridge will help.

Sweet Omelette

If you have an egg in the box and a spoonful of jam in the bottom of the jar, then you have a pudding. I would not suggest cooking more than one of these at once as they are best eaten within seconds of leaving the pan. After a reasonably substantial supper one omelette will probably serve two. Probably the best I have ever eaten was when I had some cold poached rhubarb knocking around to fill it with.

MAKES 1
3 eggs, separated
1 tablespoon caster sugar
knob of butter

Put the egg yolks into a mixing bowl with the sugar and beat until thick. A matter of seconds with an electric whisk, a little longer by hand. Beat the egg whites into stiff peaks and fold into the egg yolk and sugar with a metal spoon or spatula.

Melt the butter in your trusty omelette pan, the one that doesn't stick, and when it starts to fizz swoosh in the egg mixture. Cook over a medium heat until set on the bottom, then either put it under a preheated hot grill to cook the top a little or into a hot oven (the grill will be quicker and take only a few seconds). Add the filling of your choice (see opposite) and fold the omelette in half. Slide it out of the pan – it may need a good shove with a spatula – and eat while hot and fluffy.

Good Things to Put in Your Sweet Omelette

* A good sprinkling of sugar, perhaps from the vanilla jar

* Warmed cherry jam, the sharpish morello variety rather than the bubblegum-black-cherry one. You will need 2 or 3 tablespoons per omelette

* Crushed red berries tarted up with a glug from the Cassis bottle

* Apple slices, fried in a little butter and sugar till golden, sprinkled with a few anise seeds

The Crêpe see also page 35–6

The French don't eat crêpes from street stalls, I have been told, only tourists do. And yet the best ones I have come across were in Paris, tucked behind the Rue Mouffetard street market, where the pavement was congested with French students eating golden crêpes from white paper. Perhaps the person who told me thinks that the British no longer eat fish and chips in the street either. He should come to Islington on a Friday night.

Made at home, crêpes are one of the quickest hot puddings if you do nothing fancy with them. They are not difficult if you get the batter right and have a pan you can trust, though your first one or two may glue themselves to it. These crêpes are the cook's perk, incidentally, to be wolfed while you attempt a third.

Sophie Grigson went into great detail about making crêpes one Saturday in her compulsive column in *The Independent*. The recipe below is hers, and is the best I have come across for thin, French crêpes. They also taste of something, which is more than you can say for most. I have parted company with her when it comes to resting the batter, my impatience getting the better of me.

Thin French Crêpes

MAKES 10 CRÊPES/FOR 3–4

50g / 2oz butter

100g / 4oz plain flour

pinch of salt

1 tablespoon caster sugar

1 large egg, lightly beaten

1 egg yolk

350ml / 12fl oz milk

1½ tablespoons brandy

2 teaspoons orange flower
  water

butter, for greasing

Melt the butter in a small pan, remove from the heat and pour into a cup to cool. (It will take an age to cool in the hot pan.) Sift the flour with the salt. Mix in the sugar. Make a well in the centre and add the egg and egg yolk, plus the melted butter, which should have cooled a bit by now.

Start stirring, gradually drawing in the flour, and adding the milk to give a smooth batter. Stir in the brandy and flower water.

This is where Sophie rests her batter so that the 'starch will be almost completely gelatinised, and the batter will be able to carry a greater quantity of liquid. That means you can thin it a little more to make lighter pancakes.' The words that caught my eye, though, were, 'As soon as the batter is made up, the starch in the flour begins to swell, which means you can use it straight away.'

Cooking the Pancakes

Brush a heavy-based frying pan, or crêpe pan if you have such a thing, with a little butter. (My own small crêpe pan now has such a well-established non-stick layer built up on it that I can put it in the dishwasher and it still doesn't stick.) Put it over a medium heat until the butter melts and breaks out into tiny bubbles.

Pour in a ladleful of batter, then swirl it round the pan by rolling the pan from side to side until the base is covered in a thin layer. Pour any extra back into the batter bowl. Place over the heat and cook for a minute or so before lifting the edge of the pancake from the pan with a palette knife and peeping to see if the underside is golden brown in patches. If it is, loosen the pancake with the knife, then lift it over on to the other side. This will take less time to cook. Turn the cooked crêpe on to a plate and carry on till you have ten pancakes.

Half a Dozen Good Things to Do with a Crêpe

* Citrus juices: mix freshly squeezed lemon, orange and lime juices and sweeten with a little runny honey (you won't need very much). Drizzle them over the pancakes while still hot

* Spiced butters: soften some unsalted butter in a small pan, then spike with sweet spices, freshly ground if possible. Suitable contenders are cinnamon, cardamom and nutmeg

* Flower waters: sprinkle each hot pancake with orange flower or rosewater, dress with a dash of fresh orange juice and eat while hot

* Apple purée: spread with liberal quantities of rough apple purée, see page 42

* Melted chocolate: use the darkest chocolate you can find, softened in a bowl

* Honey and nuts: runny honey is best if you don't want to tear your pancake to shreds. Nuts should be broken up a little and toasted till golden and fragrant

* Squeeze of lemon: you can't beat a squeeze of fresh lemon juice. And that doesn't mean the stuff in the plastic yellow lemon

Clafoutis

You can't cook a clafoutis in half-an-hour, but so absurdly simple is the method (whizz it up, pour it in a pan and bake it) that I include it here in the hope that you can prepare the rest of the meal while the clafoutis cooks.

Clafoutis is little more than a sweet version of Yorkshire pudding, usually dotted with cherries or apples. It is another one on the list for those who, if they are to eat puddings at all, want them to be hot, traditional and substantial.

FOR 4

4 eggs	225ml / 8fl oz single cream
75g / 3oz plain flour	225ml / 8fl oz full cream milk
good pinch of salt	fruit of your choice, see below
75g / 3oz caster sugar	

Butter a 25cm / 10 inch tart tin, baking tin or roasting dish. Whizz all the ingredients, apart from the fruit, in the blender or food processor, or beat them all together with a hand-held whisk.

Put the fruit in the bottom of the pan, pour over the batter and bake in a preheated oven at 200°C/400°F (gas mark 6). It is done when well-risen, golden and firm, probably about 40 minutes. Sprinkle with caster sugar before eating.

Pear Clafoutis
Peel, slice and core 450g / 1lb ripe pears. Toss the slices in a little eau de vie before putting them in the buttered pan.

Cherry Clafoutis
The classic fruit to use in this batter pudding. You will need 450g / 1lb cherries for a 4-egg clafoutis. Bottled red cherries, particularly those in brandy, are particularly good here.

Fig Clafoutis
Slice 6 figs in half through the stalk. Roll each half in runny honey then put in the buttered pan.

Prune Clafoutis
Soaked prunes or the very soft French ones, rolled in brandy, make one of the best flavoured fillings. Scatter a few flaked almonds over the top just before baking. Serve warm with sugar and cream. You will need about 350g / 12oz stoned prunes, which is 450g / 1lb before stoning.

* A glass of brandy of some sort or another works well with a hot, sugary batter pudding. Calvados would be my choice, though almost anything would be suitable

PINEAPPLES

The less you do to pineapple the better. A little alcohol, in the form of Kirsch or Cointreau, or perhaps rum, or a companionable fruit such as passion fruit or orange, is all I will offer here. A truly ripe pineapple needs no embellishment.

Choose a pineapple that is heavy for its size. It should have a noticeable pineapple smell that should hit you from several inches away. To check for ripeness pull a leaf from its crown. If it comes easily then the fruit is ripe, if not put it back for another day.

In theory the core is indigestible and is usually removed. I rarely do so. If the fruit is deeply ripe then the core will be perfectly edible, though it may have a little more crispness to it. The real point of a pineapple is its juice. It must be sweet and copious. You must choose your fruit very carefully.

You can find pineapples in good condition from late autumn till May or June. They seem to lose their real magic only in high summer. But there is enough other fruit around at that time anyway. Pineapples are at their best when there is little else around, making them twice as welcome as they would be in the summer. Much of the fruit we see in the shops comes from the West Indies or Hawaii, and very good it is too.

Lately there has been an influx of miniature pineapples. They are easier to carry home, though slightly more expensive. Flown in from Indonesia mostly, these little fruit never seem to achieve the same heaviness of perfume and juiciness of flesh of their more majestic sisters. I do, though, find them ideal for one person – a large fruit can last just that bit too long if you are devouring it by yourself. Mind you, it will keep, cut side covered with film, in the fridge for a day or two.

The Tinned Stuff

Some people swear by tinned pineapple. I am not sure I agree. It is such a pale shadow of the fresh fruit, and somehow so limp and flaccid. For emergencies only, though I will concede it is a more successful candidate for canning than the strawberry. But then, isn't everything?

Ananas au Kirsch

The epitome of the Parisian bistro dessert. A joy when the fruit is perfectly ripe and the eau de vie is one of the finest. I have tasted this treatment of pineapple in a boisterous bistro close to a favourite building of mine, the Institut du Monde Arabe in Paris, the exact location of which has disappeared in a fug of Fleurie. I will find it again, though. The pineapple was sublime, even if it was only a taster from a friend's plate. I had succumbed to something altogether more hedonistic – icebergs of poached meringue floating in a dish of vanilla-scented custard.

FOR 4, AT LEAST
1 medium pineapple, absolutely ripe (see page 105)
2 tablespoons Kirsch

Peel the pineapple if you wish, though the skin is easy enough to remove as you eat. Slice the pineapple into thick slices, almost, I suggest, 2.5cm / 1 inch thick. Put two slices, a large and a small one, on each plate. Upend the Kirsch over the fruit and leave for 10 minutes or so before eating.

* If the pineapple is not quite as juicy as you would wish it to be, then sprinkle a little caster sugar over it after adding the Kirsch

* Cointreau, the orange-based liqueur, can be used instead of Kirsch, as can rum, for those who like the stuff

BANANAS *see also pages 71–2, 74–5, 96, 98, 177–8*

Bananas are a trusty friend to the short-of-time cook. Reliable, ubiquitous, cheap and satisfying, this is one fruit that never lets you down. It is simple to gauge ripeness and quality just by looking at the skin. I prefer a slightly underripe banana for eating and cooking so I tend to gravitate towards long, perfect specimens with little or no brown markings and green tinges at the stalk ends. Banana connoisseurs are more likely to head for brown-freckled ones, whose skins feel thinner and have no green about them. They will be sweeter this way, and the flavour will be deeper.

It is very easy to take bananas for granted. Any corner shop will offer a hand of the fruit in one condition or another. Rarely are they disappointing. Bananas hate the cold and in deepest winter they may suffer from too cold a storage temperature and be slightly grey inside, but this can be detected too by a slight grey tone to the yellow skin. Store your fruit in the fridge and it will turn black on you. Banana experts say that spring is the best time for quality, though I find them one of the more trustworthy fruits all year round.

As effortless desserts go, the banana takes some beating. Grilled or baked, without even so much as peeling, you will get a rich, creamy result in 20 minutes or so. Eaten hot from the oven, only a jug of cream or the flesh from a passion fruit will be needed to turn such simplicity into a memorable pudding. Sliced raw into thick yoghurt and stirred with flower honey, the banana offers an ending to a meal that will please even the most neurotic of healthy eaters. Grilled with citrus juice and spices, it will placate the most hedonistic, while simply peeled and eaten on the run, monkey-style, it should please everyone but the pretentious.

Friends of the banana include cream in all its forms, thick Greek-style yoghurt, citrus fruits, particularly lime, and spices such as cardamom and nutmeg. I am far from convinced about chocolate and bananas, though I am assured that sliced banana with hot chocolate sauce can be heavenly. But then, is there anything that could better a properly made banana custard? I think not.

Jacket Bananas

Bake unpeeled fruit in a preheated oven, 180°C/350°F (gas mark 5), till the skins are black and soft, about 25 minutes. Split the skins and pour a little cream inside. Eat the cold cream and the hot bananas from their jackets with a teaspoon.

Baked Banana with Cardamom and Orange

FOR 4

4 ripe bananas, peeled	2 cardamom pods
4 tablespoons brown sugar	juice of 1 large orange
50g / 2oz butter	

Cut the bananas into slices about 1cm / ½ inch thick. Put them into a baking dish, sprinkle with sugar and dot the butter, in little pieces, on top.

Bake the bananas for 7–8 minutes, depending on their ripeness, in a preheated oven, 200°C/400°F (gas mark 6). While the bananas are baking, remove the little black cardamom seeds from their husks and crush them roughly. If you do not have a pestle and mortar, then put them in a paper bag and bash them gently with the end of a rolling pin.

When the bananas are hot and have softened somewhat, take them out of the oven, scatter with the crushed cardamom and sprinkle over the orange juice. Return to the oven for 1 minute. Serve immediately.

Grilled Bananas

Lynda Brown, the gardener-cook, shares my passion for bananas. She grills hers unpeeled, no doubt in an attempt to contain all their sweet goodness.

'Place your banana, unpeeled, on a tin or in a fireproof dish and grill under a hot grill for about 7–10 minutes, during which the skin will blacken and the juice ooze out to form its own delicious sauce. Tear off a strip of the skin and eat the flesh with a spoon, not forgetting to scrape up all the sauce.'

* See also Banana Custard, page 96

Hot Banana Brioche

Yoghurt would be my immediate choice to lubricate this favourite fruit toast, but I have been known to go quite over the top and serve it with banana custard.

FOR 4

4 slices of brioche or *panettone*, 1cm / ½ inch thick
rum, which is quite optional
4 ripe bananas, peeled

juice of ½ orange
thick, Greek-style yoghurt, to serve

Preheat the grill until it is very hot. Put the slices of brioche or *panettone* on the grill pan. Sprinkle with rum if you wish. Slice the bananas as thick as pound coins and lay them, slightly overlapping, on top of the bread.

Squeeze over the orange juice and place the bread under the grill, until the banana starts to turn golden brown, about 5–7 minutes. Serve hot with thick yoghurt.

Foil-baked Bananas with Apricot Sauce

FOR 4
4 ripe bananas, peeled
1 × 400g / 14oz tin apricots

You will need 4 pieces of aluminium foil, each large enough to be folded around a banana.

Place the foil on the work surface. Place a banana on each one, then bring up the sides of the foil to make little packets for the fruit. Whizz the apricots to a purée in a blender or processor with a little of their canning syrup.

Spoon the purée into the little parcels and seal thoroughly by scrunching together the foil along the top. Bake in a preheated oven, 200°C/400°F (gas mark 6), for about 20 minutes. (Open one slightly and test with a skewer.) Serve hot, and let everyone open up their own parcel, which will be full of fruit-scented steam.

Grilled Bananas with Citrus and Spices

I can't remember exactly where this recipe came from or why it is in my tatty, handwritten cookbook. It originally had cardamom in it too, but on trying it again I felt something had to go. It could have been either of the other spices.

FOR 4

4 large, firm bananas	**a pinch of ground coriander**
juice of 1 lime	**40g / 1½ oz butter**
50ml / 2fl oz orange juice	**icing sugar**
a pinch of ground nutmeg	**2 tablespoons flaked almonds**

Peel the bananas and cut them in half lengthways. Put them in a shallow ovenproof dish, on a baking sheet, flat side up. Mix together the juices and spoon them over the bananas. Mix the spices with the butter and place blobs of it over the fruit.

Cook under a preheated grill till the bananas are golden and tender, about 6 minutes. Pull the dish out from the heat, dust with icing sugar and scatter over the flaked almonds. Put back under the grill till slightly browned. Eat warm.

Hot Banana Pudding

An unusual sounding method with a pleasing, almost soufflé-like result, though the colour is not as pretty as it could be. Unless you are particularly fond of beige. It is just the thing for a chilly March evening, and most of the ingredients will probably be knocking around anyway.

FOR 2, GENEROUSLY

100ml / 4fl oz double cream
½ vanilla pod or 1 teaspoon
   vanilla extract
50g / 2oz caster sugar
3 large egg yolks beaten till
   thick and creamy

3 very ripe bananas, whizzed to
  a smooth pulp
3 large egg whites
2 teaspoons lemon juice

Beat the cream with a whisk until thick and creamy. It should be sloppy, not yet capable of standing in peaks. Slit the vanilla pod in half and scrape the little black seeds into the cream or add the vanilla extract. Mix well, then fold into the cream with the egg yolks and sugar and the pulped bananas. Continue beating till thick and creamy. A matter of seconds with an electric beater.

Butter a 15cm / 6 inch soufflé dish or similar ovenproof dish and sprinkle a little sugar over it. Beat the egg whites with an electric or hand whisk till they stand in stiff peaks, then fold them gently and thoroughly into the cream. Stir in the lemon juice. Scoop the mixture gently into the buttered dish and bake in a preheated oven at 180°C/350°F (gas mark 5) till puffed and risen, about 20 minutes or so. The outside should be golden brown and risen almost to the rim of the dish, the inside creamy and scented with banana and vanilla.

Bananas with Butter and Brown Sugar

Bananas are sweet enough, and rarely need sugar. But when baked in this manner, with lime juice (you can use a lemon if that is what you have) and butter, they take on a velvety consistency and a rich flavour.

FOR 4

butter, somewhere between
30 and 50g / 1 and 2oz
4 large, ripe but firm bananas

3 tablespoons soft brown sugar, not muscovado
juice of 1 lime or ½ lemon

Butter a shallow baking dish. Peel the bananas and cut them in half lengthways. Squeeze them into the dish; they should nestle up to one another. Dot a little more butter over the fruit, then sprinkle with brown sugar. Squeeze over the lime juice and bake for 15 minutes, maybe a bit longer, in a preheated oven, 180°C/350°F (gas mark 5). Serve with cream.

Banana Yoghurt Fool

FOR 2

4 soft, ripe bananas, peeled
275g / 10oz thick, creamy, natural yoghurt

Drop the bananas in the blender and whizz till smooth, but stop before they turn gummy. Add a spoonful of yoghurt if they refuse to move, or use a food processor. Scrape into a bowl with a rubber spatula, fold in the remaining yoghurt, which should be chilled and thick, spoon into wineglasses and chill till you are ready to eat.

Bananas and Tinned Cream

Nestlé make tins of thick cream. I am not talking about condensed or evaporated milk, but thick white cream in a blue and white tin.

Normally shunning such a product in favour of the fresh stuff, I have to say that it has a certain affinity for being spooned over sliced, slightly underripe bananas. Or is that just misplaced nostalgia?

Bananas with Cream and Kirsch

As always, omit the vanilla if the stuff you have is 'essence' rather than true vanilla extract.

FOR 2

2 large, ripe bananas
lemon juice
4 tablespoons double cream

2 teaspoons Kirsch
½ teaspoon vanilla extract

Peel the bananas and slice them thickly. Put them in a bowl with a sprinkling of lemon juice. Whip the cream lightly so that it has a barely pourable consistency, stir in the Kirsch and vanilla. Scrape the cream into the dish with the bananas, and toss very gently so as not to damage the fruit. Spoon into glasses and serve – with a crisp almondy biscuit perhaps.

Blueberry and Banana Salad

Slice a few bananas, toss in a handful of blueberries and squirt over a little lemon juice. Eat immediately.

CREAMS AND CREAM CHEESES

I am not a fan of those cheeses labelled cream or curd cheese. I list below other possibilities, altogether more interesting.

Mascarpone   *see also pages 43, 53–4, 169, 172*
Cream cheese used to mean a rather yellow, bland and crumbly curd cheese sold from large tubs at the deli counter. Invariably used for cheesecakes, it had a faintly sour taste, I suspect because the demand

was low. Failing that there were little foil packets of bland and crumbly white paste, equally nasty and hideously expensive to boot.

Enter Mascarpone. This Italian immigrant from Lombardy has transformed the cream cheese market overnight. It has a rich firm consistency and a certain voluptuousness. Sweet and mild, it is interesting enough to eat by the spoonful, straight from the tub. On a midnight fridge-raid I have been known to eat alternate spoonfuls with apricot conserve; at teatime it is a luxurious spread for muffins and toast, and even more special when topped with a handful of strawberries that have been sprinkled with balsamic vinegar.

Sold by the large tub, it is somewhat expensive, though tempered by the fact that a little goes a long way.

Ricotta   *see also pages 116, 172–3*

A fresh Italian cheese of which I am becoming enormously fond. I include it here on the grounds that it is a friend to the quick cook and can provide an instant dessert when served alongside perfectly ripe greengages, apricots and figs. One of the most versatile of cheeses, it can be whizzed into cream puddings to be flavoured with brandy or rum, stirred through with chopped peel or dark chocolate chips. Use within a couple of days of purchase as it does not keep well, and left carelessly wrapped (here speaks the voice of experience again) it will pick up every flavour in the fridge. It also has the advantage of being the cheapest of the lot.

Fromage Frais

This can be substituted in many of the recipes where Mascarpone is mentioned. It stars as an essential ingredient in fools and fruit desserts, and as such it is hard to beat, offering the creaminess of its high-fat sisters without the richness. In its purest form a fresh curd cheese, it is more often than not mixed with cream, resulting in a thicker, richer and more delectable cheese. Most supermarkets offer tubs of *fromage frais* with their fat percentage clearly marked. The low fat ones are softer and to my mind, less interesting. In summer an instant pudding can be made by serving a little bowl of *fromage frais* topped with finely chopped flesh from a melon or puréed berries. A sprig of mint or even a little flower would be quite harmonious with such a delicate, summery pot.

Low Fat Products

A word about products labelled low fat or light or 'lite'. Generally speaking and without getting boringly technical, these products are the basic high fat version made lighter with the addition of air and water. Of course, a pot of cream cheese will be lighter in fat if a third of the tub is nothing more than air, it's what gives 'lite' products their characteristic whipped texture. There are some very well-known corporate giants whose food empires are built on little more than air, water and hype. Interestingly, the French, who embraced the low fat dairy product like a nation possessed, have recently lost interest in such stuff in favour of the real thing. And they can still boast one of the lowest rates of cardiac arrest in the world. Or so I am told.

Crema alla Mascarpone

A somewhat addictive and slightly alcoholic cream, which is only fractionally more effort than one of those instant whip things.

FOR 4

2 eggs, separated	275g / 10oz Mascarpone cheese
50g / 2oz caster sugar	1 tablespoon brandy or Kirsch

Cream the egg yolks with the sugar for a few seconds, then add the Mascarpone and beat till light and creamy. A matter of minutes with an electric whisk. Stir in the brandy or Kirsch.

Wash the beaters, then whisk the egg whites till stiff. Fold them into the cream, gently but thoroughly, with a metal spoon. Spoon into glasses and chill for as long as you can, 20 minutes at the least. The cream will thicken slightly.

Mascarpone with Prunes and Almonds

Prunes and cream cheese are a classic combination. They usually manifest themselves as prunes stuffed with cottage cheese, which is fine, but a better variation to my mind is Mascarpone cheese served with a prune purée. I have seen jars of the purée but not often enough to include in a recipe, so suggest that you make your own with either prunes soaked in brandy or those plump and moist fruits from Agen in France. They are not so hard to find nowadays.

FOR 4

225g / 8oz prunes soaked in brandy

1 tablespoon apple juice or water, if necessary

175g / 6oz Mascarpone cheese

12 whole almonds

Cut the prunes in half and remove the stones. Liquidise the fruit in a blender, adding 1 tablespoon of apple juice or water if it seems rather dry. The consistency needs to be that of a thick purée. Place scoops of Mascarpone on each of four small plates, then spoon some of the purée on to each one. Split each almond into approximately four slivers and scatter them over the cheese and purée.

Gingered Ricotta

Golden, translucent knobs of stem ginger in syrup are a useful delicacy to have in the cupboard. Here they add a somewhat luxurious element to a simple mixture of low fat cream cheeses and almonds.

FOR 2

100g / 4oz Ricotta cheese

4 tablespoons *fromage frais*

1 tablespoon caster sugar

2 tablespoons ground almonds

2 lumps of stem ginger in syrup

2 tablespoons syrup from the ginger jar

brandy snaps, to serve

Push the Ricotta through a sieve with a wooden spoon and stir in the *fromage frais*. Stir in the sugar and almonds. Cut the knobs of ginger into small dice, about as big as dolly mixtures, then stir into the Ricotta with the syrup.

Chill for at least 20 minutes so that the flavours blend, then serve in tiny pots with brandy snaps to dip.

Fromage Blanc

A lovely, softly piquant cream of which I am particularly fond. Its soft consistency and gentle tartness could not be more flattering to fruits (I am thinking of summer berries here), though I am happy enough to indulge in a whole small bowl of it all to myself.

FOR 4
225g / 8oz thick, Greek-style yoghurt
225ml / 8fl oz double cream
3 egg whites

Put the yoghurt, which must be of the strained variety, in a large bowl. In another one, beat the cream with a hand or electric whisk, until it forms soft peaks. It should not be too stiff. Fold the cream into the yoghurt gently and thoroughly with a metal spoon. Beat the egg whites till stiff. Fold them into the cream and yoghurt, then chill for 15 minutes. Serve in little pots or cups with a teaspoon.

* Grind a little nutmeg over the cream; a quite delightful addition

* Put a few dark berries, such as blackberries or loganberries, into a serving bowl. Crush them lightly with a fork till they bleed purple juice, then spoon over some of the *fromage blanc*. Stir gently, just enough to streak the cream with purple

* Serve in small bowls with a little (and I mean a little) demerara sugar

* Stir a little fruit preserve, apricot, quince or fig perhaps, into the cheese. Eat piled on to little water biscuits

STAPLES AND STODGE

A water biscuit and a slice of fruit is not my idea of heaven on a cold evening. I want something satisfying, comforting and hot after my trudge home and quickly made storecupboard supper. Steaming bowls of sleep-inducing stodge are much more my style. Rice and cornmeal are the two storecupboard staples I continually rely on for quick hot puddings. They keep well in air-tight kilner jars and are both frugal and satisfying in the extreme.

Don't believe anyone who tells you rice pudding isn't fast food. Creamy rice puddings scented in Middle Eastern style with rosewater and spiked with pistachios are perhaps my favourite examples of sweet comfort food, and can be knocked together in no time at all. A bowl of *gnocchi*, sticky and golden and smelling softly of vanilla and lemon, is just as fast and to me is the most welcome of all.

The Twenty-minute Rice Pudding

A creamy rice pudding in less time than it takes to heat up a ready-made one. There are tinned ones, of course, but the rice is too soft and pappy. Pudding or *arborio* (risotto) rice is essential if the grains are to swell up in juicy fashion.

FOR 4

8 heaped tablespoons *arborio* or pudding rice
300ml / ½ pint milk
300ml / ½ pint double cream

a vanilla pod, split in half lengthways or 1 teaspoon vanilla extract
6 tablespoons water
large knob of butter
4 tablespoons caster sugar

Put the rice in a medium-sized, heavy-based pan, then pour in the milk, cream, vanilla pod or extract and water. Bring to the boil over a medium heat, then turn down the flame until the milk is bubbling gently, just as you would have it for a risotto.

Let it cook for 15–20 minutes until the rice has swelled with the milk. It should be soft when done, but not without a little bite. Add the butter, no more than an ounce, whip out the vanilla pod, and stir in the sugar. As soon as the sugar has dissolved, the pudding is ready.

How to get a Crispy Skin on your Fast Rice Pudding

Connoisseurs of rice pudding demand a crisp skin that is golden brown all over. Rice-pudding-skin bores will also insist on a patch of dark brown skin that is swollen and on the verge of being charred.

After stirring in the sugar, scrape the pudding into a heat-proof serving dish. Get the grill really hot then place the pudding under the grill, about 2.5cm / 1 inch away from the heat.

Grill for 3 or 4 minutes, until the skin is golden brown in most parts, dark brown in others.

Rice Pudding with Rosewater, Cardamom and Pistachio

A classic from Afghanistan that I first encountered in Norfolk, at Ruth and David Watson's pub, the Fox and Goose at Fressingfield, Suffolk. Known affectionately as the Effing G., this is one of those country pubs with good food and the sort of bar where you can doze off of an afternoon in a squashy chair. This is my version of their recipe, which is in turn a version of Jeremy Round's. They also make a mean onion bhaji, but that is another matter.

8 heaped tablespoons *arborio* or
  pudding rice
300ml / ½ pint milk
300ml / ½ pint double cream
6 tablespoons water
a vanilla pod, split in half
  lengthways or 1 teaspoon
  vanilla extract

1 teaspoon cardamom pods
2 handfuls of pistachio nuts in
  their shells
4 tablespoons caster sugar, and
  perhaps a little more
4 teaspoons rosewater

Follow the recipe on pages 118–19 with the rice, milk, cream, water and vanilla. While the rice is cooking, remove the pods from the cardamom seeds and shells from the pistachios. Grind the cardamoms to a powder in the coffee grinder, using a pestle and mortar or with the aid of a rolling pin and a small plastic bag. Chop the pistachios roughly.

Stir the sugar into the rice, and you had better take out the vanilla pod if you used one as well, then add the ground cardamom. Stir in the rosewater. Cook for a further minute, then taste the pudding. Add more sugar – I think this dish should be really quite sweet – and more rosewater if you like. Serve while still warm and creamy, in two small bowls, scattered with the chopped green pistachios.

* I once added a few pieces of gold leaf to the last dish. Just peeled from the backing paper in little bits and sprinkled over the pudding. It was an absolutely charming addition and, surprisingly, not as pretentious as you might expect. Gold leaf, in little books, is available from art shops and Indian grocers. And is fearfully expensive

Five Nice Rice Puddings

Cinnamon Rice

To the basic rice pudding recipe on pages 118–19 (not the rosewater one), add a pinch or two of ground cinnamon and grate in a little nutmeg at the start of cooking.

Orange Flower Water Rice Pudding
In the Middle East they are very fond, so I gather, of adding orange blossom water to their sweet rice, in much the same way as in India they use rosewater. Follow either the basic rice pudding recipe or, even better, the scented one, adding orange flower water in place of the rosewater.

Rice Pudding and Jam
Forget school dinners. Sweet rice, thick and creamy, can be really good with a blob of decent jam. The trick is not to be tempted to stir it in too thoroughly; just stir the jam enough to streak the rice with purple or red rather than to turn it a monotone hideous pink. It is the subtlety of a mixed mouthful of tart jam and unctuous creamy rice that is worth eating.

Best jams for stirring into rice pudding are blackcurrant, apricot or rhubarb, because their slight tartness is more welcome swirled into the bland creamy mass than the ubiquitous sweet and sticky strawberry.

Saffron Rice Pudding
Add a couple of pinches of saffron powder (the contents of one of those little sachets) to the base recipe with a little ground cinnamon when you add the milk and cream to the rice. A squeeze of lemon at the end of cooking will not go amiss.

Rice Pudding with Orange Zest and Ginger

My unauthentic version of an Iranian-style rice pudding.

FOR 2

1 small carrot, grated coarsely
grated zest of 1 small orange
2 tablespoons golden raisins
2 tablespoons flaked almonds

2 knobs of stem ginger in syrup
a little syrup from the ginger
   jar

Make the rice as in the basic recipe on pages 118–19. Add the grated carrot, orange zest and raisins when you add the sugar, then they will keep their sparkle. Toast the almonds till golden under a hot grill or in a non-stick frying pan.

When the rice is cooked, divide it between two small dishes and scatter the toasted almonds on top. Chop the knobs of ginger into dice, add them in a small heap on top of the rice and drizzle with a little of the syrup.

Sweet Gnocchi

Sustaining, soothing and mildly soporific, this is surely the most comforting pudding of all. The pudding eater's answer to mashed potatoes or perhaps *aligot*. It will not amuse gâteau fanciers and their kind who would no doubt blanch if given a bowl of the sweet yellow mush, even if served piping hot and softly scented with lemon and vanilla.

The term *gnocchi* is confusing here; perhaps sweet polenta would have been more accurate. It may have helped convey the extraordinarily frugal and nannying quality of such a pudding. Whatever you call it, it is a quick hot pudding made with sugar, fine cornmeal or rice flour, milk and eggs. This is a simple dish that will be ruined by second-rate ingredients. Choose a fine cornmeal rather than the coarser varieties, which will give a grainy texture not wanted here. More than ever, it is essential to use the finest vanilla extract rather than the nasty essences around.

The recipe came to me via Matthew Fort, the Food Editor of the *Guardian*, who in turn procured it from Francesco Zanchetta, the chef at Riva in Barnes. Matthew serves it Riva-style, that is, left to cool then cut into shapes and baked with a honey and Marsala syrup (see page 124). I have stopped halfway through his recipe, and offer it as a rib-sticking golden mush for a chilly spring evening.

FOR 2

2 egg yolks
150g / 5oz caster sugar
a heavy 30g / 1oz rice flour
grated zest of 1 small lemon (or
   ½ large one)

vanilla extract
300ml / ½ pint milk

Beat the egg yolks and the sugar with a small whisk or electric beater till light and creamy. Beat in the rice flour, grated lemon and vanilla extract. Pour in the milk and continue beating or whisking till all is amalgamated. Check there are no lumps at the bottom of the bowl.

Pour into a medium-sized, heavy-based saucepan – non-stick would be good for this – and place over a medium heat. Bring to the boil, stirring every few seconds or so, then turn down to a simmer. Continue stirring, almost continually now. It will suddenly change from a thin yellow liquid with lumps to a rich, thick custard. Keep stirring, paying special attention to the corners, for 3 minutes until it has thickened.

Divide between two small serving dishes, allow to cool very slightly, and eat while still warm.

* Spoon a gloop of liquid honey on top. Chestnut honey is the one I use. Partially stir it in as you eat

* Forget the 'allow to cool very slightly' and eat it steaming hot, dipping each spoonful of pudding first into a dish of cold milk, then into the sugar bowl

* Open up that tin of vacuum-packed chestnuts that has been sitting in the cupboard for weeks. Scatter the contents on a baking sheet and grill till sizzling. Chop coarsely, then stir into the golden mush

Gnocchi *with Honey, Marsala and Butter Sauce*

This is my version of what I ate at Matthew Fort's. Which is his version of what he ate at Riva.

Follow the previous recipe until it tells you to spoon the mixture into bowls. Don't do that. Scrape it out on to a buttered plate instead. Smooth it with the back of the spoon to a thickness of about 1cm / ½ inch. Leave to cool. It won't take long, about 20 minutes.

Melt 2 tablespoons of runny honey with 2 tablespoons of Marsala in a small saucepan over a medium heat. Whisk in a lump of cold butter, a heavy ounce (30g), and bring to the boil. Remove from the heat, and cover with a lid.

Cut the paste into squares or diamond shapes, probably about eight to ten. With help from a palette knife or spatula, lift them on to a very lightly buttered baking sheet. Brush with a small amount of melted butter and bake in a preheated oven, 200°C/400°F (gas mark 6), for 8 minutes. They will be slightly puffed and soft to handle.

Take them out of the oven, scoop each one up carefully with a palette knife and arrange on two large plates. Pour over some of the warm Marsala sauce. Enough for two.

* A small ripe pear, peeled if you can be bothered, and sliced thinly, can be warmed through in the honey and Marsala and served alongside the *gnocchi*

* I haven't tried it, but I dare say a peach, sliced into eighths and heated in the boozy, buttery syrup, would be very fine here too

ICE CREAM *see also pages 36–7, 80, 89*

I have spent many a happy hour making ice cream. I was given a little machine some time ago that turns a strawberry purée and some sugar syrup into the most sublime *sorbet de fraise* in half an hour or so. Particularly if I slop in a couple of spoonfuls of thick yoghurt before it has finished. Before the machine I used to make it in the freezer, taking the mixture out every hour or so to stir it as it froze. That was when I had a deepfreeze. And the time to do it.

At the weekend from early spring to late autumn I use my machine, though it is better at sorbet than creamy ice. During the week I am happy to buy my ice cream from the shops, and always like to have a tub in the freezer box at the top of the fridge. Usually vanilla. There is little wrong with bought ice cream. The smart American-style ones are really quite good, though I must say I find them too sweet and their texture boringly consistent. What I would really like to get hold of are the ices of my childhood, the ones made by small dairies.

Those ices had character, they were more milky than creamy, and were a treat to be enjoyed on shopping trips, when my parents would take me out to tea in a department store. I can clearly remember the strawberry ices in their little silver dishes with condensation running down the outside. Now that was ice cream. Replaced in later years with the household brands we know so well, made with vegetable fat instead of dairy produce and hardly worthy of the name ice cream.

* You can only make good ice cream with good ingredients. Vegetable fat is not one of them. For the best ice cream look out for those which contain cream, sugar and eggs

A Few Good Things to Pour, Scatter or Spoon Over Ice Cream . . .

* Maple syrup: make sure that what you are buying is the real thing; avoid bottles with labels that say Maple Flavour Syrup. Particularly suitable for coffee and walnut ices

* Chocolate shavings: peel curls or shavings of chocolate from a bitter bar with a vegetable peeler. Easiest when taken from the flat of the bar and when the chocolate is at room temperature. Best for vanilla or coffee ices

* Crunchy muesli: crunchy oats and dried fruit are a surprisingly good topping for vanilla and chocolate ices

* Toasted nuts: the secret is to toast the nuts till golden. Let them burn and they will be bitter. A sprinkling of sugar before toasting, particularly over almonds, is unnecessary but satisfyingly crunchy. Flaked almonds are best with strawberry ices, walnuts (toasted, then rubbed to remove some of their papery skins) with coffee, and hazelnuts (same treatment, then toasted again) over chocolate

* Pistachios: shelled and chopped, no need to toast, scattered over strawberry ices

* Brittle, *turrón* and *praline*: Glistening shards of nuts in glassy caramel add an exhilarating crunch. Crush with a rolling pin or bang with a hammer. Best of all as partners for berry ices and sorbets

* Smarties: a sweet, childishly indulgent crunch to scatter over vanilla ices

* Chocolate sauce: see page 129

* Fruits in alcohol: a jar of fruits preserved in alcohol and a tub of ice cream is one of the most delectable desserts I can think of, particularly if the ice cream is vanilla and the fruit is pears in eau de vie. Cherries in brandy and prunes in Armagnac are easy to find at good food shops and can be stored almost indefinitely. A first-class storecupboard pudding

And Sorbets . . .

* Generally speaking, sorbets do not respond favourably to embellishment, though a shot of compatible liquor is unlikely to go amiss:
Raspberry Sorbet – eau de vie *de framboise*
Pear Sorbet – eau de vie Poire William
Lemon Sorbet – Vodka

Blackcurrant Sorbet – Cassis, an intensely fruity mouthful
Or, of course, a little of the fruit with which the sorbet has been made

Instant Raspberry Ice Cream

FOR 4
225ml / 8fl oz double cream
275g / 10oz frozen raspberries

Put the cream and the frozen fruit (it must be frozen) into the food processor or blender. Whizz on low speed till the fruit and cream form a pink creamy mass. You have ice cream.

* To save you the trouble of trying it out, this idea doesn't work with frozen blackcurrants and is not much better with strawberries. Stick to raspberries

Instant Raspberry Sorbet

Whizz a packet of frozen raspberries to slush in the food processor. Divide it quickly into wineglasses. Upend a measure of *framboise* over the result and call it raspberry sorbet.

Espresso Ice Cream

As I said earlier, I love dishes where hot and cold are played off against one another. Shockingly cold ice cream with hot, slightly bitter coffee is one that I think works especially well. Sweeten the espresso if you wish, but make sure that the two components are very cold and very hot.

FOR 2
4 large balls of vanilla or coffee ice cream
2 *demi-tasses* of hot, strong espresso coffee

Put the balls of ice cream, in pairs, into large cups or small dishes. Pour over the hot coffee and eat with a teaspoon.

The Ice Cream Sundae

People come over all sniffy about ice cream sundaes. And well they might. The average mess of tinned fruit in jelly with vegetable fat ice cream and raspberry syrup is a travesty. But a true ice cream sundae can be a thing of joy; some puréed and a few whole fresh loganberries or raspberries with vanilla ice cream or chocolate ice cream with melted bitter chocolate and coffee liqueur. Try vanilla ice cream in a tall glass with sliced fresh peaches and raspberry purée or just a glass of proper strawberry ice cream with fresh strawberries and a sauce made from the fruit sharpened with lemon juice. A good ice cream sundae is a true celebration of fine ice cream and ripe fruit. And what is wrong with that?

A Few Sundae Suggestions

Tall, thick glasses and long-handled spoons *de rigueur*

* Sliced purple figs, small scoops of Mascarpone cheese and larger ones of vanilla ice cream drizzled with raspberry purée

* Orange sorbet, the juice and seeds from a passion fruit and slices of fresh pineapple

* Vanilla ice cream, hot chocolate sauce and slices of ripe, juicy pears

* Broken meringue, softly whipped cream, vanilla ice cream and raspberries, crushed slightly with a fork. A dollop of raspberry purée (fresh berries whizzed in the blender with a teaspoon of lemon juice) wouldn't go amiss either

* Sliced bananas, neither too thin nor too ripe, vanilla ice cream, the juice and seeds of a passion fruit, with a little double cream. Go over the top with toasted flaked almonds if you want

* Prunes in brandy or Armagnac, *fromage frais* and chocolate ice cream. Tip over a measure of the prune liquor as you eat

A Few Quick Sauces for Ice Cream, Poached Fruits and Their Like

Quick Blackcurrant Sauce
Frozen blackcurrants make a wonderful sauce in more or less 10 minutes. Tip a punnet of frozen blackcurrants (they are usually sold in 225g / 8oz packs) into a stainless steel pan, add a tablespoon or two of water and a lid. Cook over gentle heat for 5–6 minutes, till they start to burst, then add sugar to taste. Spoon hot over cold ice cream, poached pears or stir into thick, Greek-style yoghurt.

Shiny Chocolate Sauce

175g / 6oz finest plain chocolate **2 tablespoons golden syrup**
50g / 2oz butter **200ml / 7fl oz milk**
50g / 2oz caster sugar

Break the chocolate into squares and melt it, with the butter, in a bowl over a pan of hot water. Stir in the sugar and syrup until dissolved, then pour in the milk and continue to cook for 10 minutes, until the sauce thickens.

Vanilla Toffee Sauce
A thick fudge sauce that for once tastes more of vanilla than sugar. The vanilla is the secret: use the finest quality vanilla extract that I bang on about in the introduction, rather than 'essence'.

50g / 2oz butter **vanilla extract**
100g / 4oz soft brown sugar **150ml / ¼ pint double cream**
100g / 4oz golden syrup

Put everything except the vanilla extract and cream into a heavy-based saucepan. Leave over a moderate heat till all has dissolved, then turn the heat up slightly and let the mixture bubble away gently for 5 minutes. No longer. Add a few drops of vanilla extract – depending on the quality you have you may need anything up to a teaspoon – then pour in the cream. Give the mixture a good stir and set aside to cool. It will thicken more quickly if you pour the sauce into a cool, but heatproof, jug. Use in sundaes, or over baked bananas.

CHOCOLATE *see also pages 49–50, 129*

Chocolate, like olive oil, is something that is taken more seriously nowadays. Some people, I venture, might even sport bars of expensive and difficult-to-obtain chocolate just as others do bottles of 'estate bottled, cold pressed, extra virgin olive oil'. Another culinary status symbol.

When I refer to chocolate in the recipes and ideas that follow I mean fine chocolate, not candy. The difference is easy to spot even before you taste it. Take two bars of chocolate, one a well-known brand name that we have known since childhood and the other a fine, more expensive bar such as, say, Valrhona or Barry. The former will break softly while the latter will snap crisply, the texture of the cheaper chocolate will be fudgey, grainy and soft. Its colour will be a pale dull brown. The fine bar will be shiny and smooth, a lovely dark, rich browny black.

Taste them. The fine stuff tastes instantly of chocolate, not sugar. But there is no real bitterness there either. There may be a faint fruitiness about it or a tinge of coffee. You will probably be left with the flavour of chocolate but your mouth will feel clean. Now taste the cheap chocolate, which I prefer to call candy. It instantly coats the roof of the mouth. It feels greasy and cloying on the palate. That is because it contains vast quantities of vegetable fat and sugar.

For puddings that taste of chocolate rather than sugar and grease you should look for chocolate that contains over 47 per cent cocoa solids. I have met some with as little as 17 per cent and as high as 90 per cent. I part company with many other writers and cooks over

Swiss chocolate, which I find too creamy, sweet and inferior to the French brands. Green and Black's, the organic chocolate, is a favourite of mine, with a deep chocolate flavour and a slight bitterness that I enjoy. Those interested in such things might note that fine chocolate contains considerably fewer calories than the cheap article.

Some of the major chain stores now stock chocolate with high cocoa solids, occasionally under own-brand labels. Beware that what you are buying is not something called 'chocolate flavour cake covering'. In my book it is one of the nastiest food products ever created and the most that can be said of it is that it is brown and sweet. Fine chocolate is available from chocolate shops, good grocers and delis. It may at first seem expensive, but it goes further as it has more flavour and the dessert you end up with will have an infinitely better taste. Like most good things, the finest chocolate can seem addictive (though some so-called 'chocoholics' may find they are actually addicted to sugar) and once hooked there is no going back to the cheap stuff. Although I have rarely known anyone refuse a finger of Kit Kat.

Chocolate for Pudding

A bar of fine chocolate is a good friend to the fast foodie. Chocolate puddings can be as simple as dipping a thin, nutty biscuit into a pot of melted chocolate, or as sophisticated as a hot chocolate soufflé. One of the most successful fast puddings I regularly offer, though something of a cheat, is a plate of different chocolate pieces. The better quality chocolates have surprisingly individual characters, and snapped into jagged shards rather than cut into neat triangles, a mixed plate always seems to go down well.

Melting Chocolate

If you want smooth, voluptuous melted chocolate, and I assume you do, it is worth taking a little care. All will end in tears if you melt your expensive chocolate over too high a heat, or stir it too much.

Break the chocolate, which will snap keenly if it is good stuff, into pieces 2.5cm / 1 inch or so square. Ignore anyone who says you need to chop it finely. Put the pieces in a heatproof china or glass bowl and set over a pan of water. The pan should be of a size that the bowl sits comfortably in the top. Put the pan over a high heat, turning the heat down as soon as the water comes to the boil (and not a minute later). The water should do little more than shudder.

Leave the chocolate alone. Do not stir it. It is ready when there are no lumps of solid chocolate left (this is not as obvious as it seems, they tend to lurk under the surface). Turn off the heat and gently stir the liquid chocolate. It will remain shiny, smooth and liquid until the water cools.

A Few Good Things to do with Melted Chocolate

* Give each diner a tiny coffee cup full of warm chocolate and a handful of things to dip in it:
  ratafia biscuits
  trifle sponges
  those Italian cigarette wafer biscuits
  slices of underripe pear
  pieces of toasted brioche

* Drizzle over peeled and thinly sliced oranges or bananas

* Pour over halved, cored and poached pears

A quick dessert that always seems to go down well is something dipped in chocolate. It takes barely 20 minutes to dry in a cool room and can continue drying while you eat the rest of your meal.

Chocolate Dipped Praline

I often serve lumps of praline dipped in chocolate instead of a pudding. Best to snap the nutty caramel into mouth-sized pieces before dipping, as they are awkward to break later. Dip each piece halfway into a pot of melted chocolate and leave on waxed paper to dry. Pile on a small plate and pass around with the coffee.

Chocolate Almonds

Take a couple of handfuls of shelled but not skinned almonds. Place in a dry frying pan and cook till fragrant. Grill them if it is easier. Let them cool and melt 100g / 4oz of fine chocolate over hot water as on pages 131–2. Toss the almonds into the chocolate and stir till they are covered.

Dust a piece of greaseproof paper generously with cocoa powder – it really must be the finest stuff – then lift each almond out of the chocolate with a small spoon and drop on to the cocoa-covered paper. Roll them gently in the cocoa and leave to cool. You will probably wish you had made more.

Ricotta with Chocolate and Cognac

The cocoa powder you use is all-important. Drinking chocolate is not the same, it contains sugar and is pretty nasty anyway. Make sure that the cocoa is better than the average; the Dutch or French brands have a superior flavour to the well-known brands.

FOR 2

4 tablespoons raisins
1 tablespoon Cognac
100g / 4oz Ricotta cheese
4 tablespoons *fromage frais*,
    quark or *petit suisse*

2 tablespoons caster sugar
2 tablespoons cocoa powder
brandy snaps or biscuits, to
    serve

Put the raisins in a cup. Pour over the Cognac and leave for 10 minutes. Push the Ricotta through a sieve into a pudding basin and stir in the *fromage frais* or whatever. Stir in the sugar and cocoa powder, then the soaked raisins and any liquid they have failed to absorb.

Chill in the fridge for 15 minutes, or longer if you have it. (Any longer than that and you should cover it to stop it getting 'fridgey'.) Serve in small pots or cups with brandy snaps or other crisp biscuits.

Bread and Chocolate: a mid morning pick-me-up

It seems the oddest of all combinations, bread and chocolate. But a light airy bap, one of the flat ones with a little flour on top, is quite delightful as a snack when split and eaten with squares of fine chocolate. I didn't believe it either till I tried it. If the fickleness of fashion has had your baker swapping his floury baps for holey Italian *ciabatta*, don't worry, it will work just as well.

* Chocolate does nothing for peaches, strawberries or kiwi fruit

Chocolate Truffle Cake

Chocolate truffle cakes fall into two main types: the ubiquitous mousse-like cake on every restaurant menu from steak houses to three star temples of gastronomy, and the slabs of rock-hard biscuit cake at the deli counter. I don't rate either of them particularly highly. Most deli cakes taste stale even when they are not and most restaurant puddings tend to leave me dead from the waist up.

The pudding that follows offers something of the professionalism and decadence of the former with the homely, biscuit addition of the latter. When I want a slice of hopelessly rich chocolate cake, and I lack the time to make Alice Waters's ultimate version from her book *Chez Panisse Desserts*, then the following recipe is the one I currently use. It was given to me by Christabel Gairdner, as if she hasn't contributed enough to this book already, and is a favourite of friends of hers.

I particularly like the idea that a pint of cream, a pound of chocolate and a packet of biscuits will give me a pudding. Even though it is the very devil to cut.

It will take you half an hour to make but you will need to allow for setting time.

FOR 8–10

225g / 8oz digestive biscuits
100g / 4oz butter
450g / 1lb finest quality
   chocolate

600ml / 1 pint double cream
cocoa powder

Lightly butter a cake tin, about 23cm / 9 inches in diameter, depending on whether you want a thick or thin cake. I prefer to use a larger diameter tin to produce a slim version. A loose-bottomed tin is pretty much essential; one of those with a spring clip will make life even easier.

Crush the biscuits in the food processor or using a rolling pin and a plastic bag. They should resemble coarse, rather than fine breadcrumbs. Melt the butter in a small pan over a medium heat. Stir in the crumbs and mix. Tip the buttered crumbs into the cake tin and press down quite firmly to give a flattish biscuit crumb base. Place in the fridge.

Melt the chocolate as described earlier (in small pieces in a bowl over a pan of simmering water, if you cannot be bothered to check back). Whip the cream to stand in firm peaks, then stir in the melted chocolate, gently but thoroughly. Spoon the chocolate cream over the crumbs and leave in the fridge till set. I have known the cake to be ready in a couple of hours, though some like to leave it overnight. Sprinkle with cocoa before serving in small pieces.

Chocolate Ginger

A dark chocolate flatters shining globes of ginger in syrup like nothing else. Mascarpone is something of a foil.

FOR EACH PERSON

a large scoop of Mascarpone cheese
3 knobs of stem ginger with a little of the bottling syrup
2 tablespoons melted fine chocolate

Place a generous scoop of Mascarpone in the middle of a small plate. Slice the ginger into pound-coin-like pieces and scatter loosely around the Mascarpone. Drizzle the melted chocolate over the whole plate and eat with a teaspoon. Coffee, strong and hot, will be welcome at this point.

Chocolate Coffee Cake

I know that this recipe barely qualifies as fast food but if there is one thing I am happy to break a few rules for it will be chocolate cake and especially one as delectable as this. Don't be put off by the fact the cake looks uncooked when you take it from the oven, it will settle down on cooling, and be distinctly squidgy in the centre, making it a candidate for dessert rather than a tea-time cake. It seems gilding the lily to suggest a little puddle of *crème fraîche* on the side, but the sharp, lactic quality of the cream takes the edge off the cake's richness.

FOR 8

180g / 6oz fine, dark chocolate, chopped
3 tablespoons very strong coffee
140g / 5oz butter, diced

5 free range eggs, separated
200g / 7oz golden caster sugar
1 teaspoon of baking powder
2 tablespoons cocoa powder
90g / 3oz plain flour

Line the base of a 21–23cm / 8–9 inch shallow spring-form cake tin with baking parchment, buttering the tin lightly to hold the paper in place.

Set the oven to 180°C/350°F (gas mark 4). Break the chocolate into small pieces and set it in a small bowl balanced over a pan of simmering water. See the 'melting chocolate' instruction on pages 132–2. As soon as the chocolate starts to soften, add the coffee and leave it for two or three minutes. Stir very gently, then, when the chocolate has melted add the butter in small chunks and stir in.

Meanwhile, beat the egg whites till they stand in peaks – this will take seconds with an electric mixer. Fold in the sugar with a metal spoon. Do this tenderly but thoroughly. Mix the baking powder with the cocoa and flour. Remove the chocolate from the heat, quickly stir in the egg yolks, then slowly, firmly and gently fold the melted chocolate into the egg whites. Lastly, sift in the flour and cocoa mixture.

Stir the mixture lovingly with a large metal spoon, taking care not to knock out any air. It should be light and wobbly. Do not over-mix – just enough to fold in the flour. Scoop the mixture into the lined tin, scraping every little bit out of the bowl with a rubber spatula. Bake in the preheated oven for 35 minutes. Leave to cool in its tin, then carefully lift out. Dust with cocoa powder if you wish, but it is not essential. Serve in small slices, on large plates, with *crème fraîche*.

Hot Chocolate Soufflé

A complete doddle. Everyone will be suitably impressed and think you are a genius. Which, of course, you are.

FOR 2 LARGE, INDIVIDUAL SOUFFLÉS

100g / 4oz fine chocolate
a little butter
50g / 2oz caster sugar

3 large eggs, separated
icing sugar, for dusting

Set the oven to 200°C/400°F (gas mark 6). Break the chocolate into bits and melt in a bowl over hot water. Follow the melting chocolate instructions on pages 131–2.

While the oven is heating and the chocolate is melting, rub a little butter round the inside of each of two soufflé dishes. They should be the large individual size, the ones that hold 350ml / 12fl oz. Or you could make four smaller ones if your soufflé dishes are tiny. Sprinkle a little of the sugar around the buttered dishes, then shake the excess back into the rest of the sugar.

Whisk the egg yolks and sugar till creamy; they don't have to be thick. A matter of seconds with an electric whisk. Rinse the beaters under the tap and dry carefully, then whisk the egg whites till they stand in stiff peaks. Remove the chocolate mixture from the heat and stir it into the egg yolks and sugar. Do this thoroughly but gently.

Working quickly, scoop half of the egg whites into the chocolate, mix gently but thoroughly, then scrape the mixture back into the egg whites. Mix carefully. A metal spoon, as large as you have, is best for this. What you want to end up with is a rich, chocolatey mixture without lumps of egg white, but mixed tenderly enough that it is still light and full of air.

Using a rubber spatula, scrape the mixture into the soufflé dishes. They should be full to within 1cm / ½ inch or so. Bake in the preheated oven for 15 minutes. They are done when they are risen, slightly spongy around the edges and creamy in the middle. Dust with icing sugar if you feel like it.

* You can look inside the oven to see if they are ready without disaster, but don't slam the oven door afterwards

* Your friends must wait for their soufflé, not the other way round. It will hold up for a minute or two, but not much more. Don't push your luck. They should be seated and ready to eat as the soufflé comes from the oven. This is really the best pudding to serve to a special friend at an informal meal in the kitchen. If you insist in doing eight of them for a dinner party you are either a masochist or trying to prove something. Don't blame me if it all ends in tears

* The inside should be really quite creamy. Cook the soufflés a little too long and you will have a more solid texture. Rather like a cake. In which case, serve them from their dish, with cream, and call them chocolate puddings

* Don't worry if your soufflés don't rise perfectly all the way round like some whizz-kid chef's. Yours may rise more on one side than the other. They may even crack a little on top. Yours will be better than the chef's perfect version. Yours will have charm. And anyway, no one likes a clever Dick

LEMONS

I feel lost without a lemon in the kitchen. From a puddings point of view, lemons are nigh on essential for adding acidity to balance the oversweet and for bringing out the flavour of some fruits and preventing the discoloration of others. They are equally useful as major ingredients in their own right.

Use them as principal flavourings for puddings where a balance of richness and piquancy is needed: a fresh-tasting syllabub, the sugar and cream given tang by lemon juice; an absurdly rich pot of *crème fraîche* and yoghurt stirred through with lemon curd and served in miniature pots; or just lemon juice as the major flavouring for crêpes hot from the pan.

Choosing Lemons

The only way to tell if a lemon is worth the money is to squeeze it. You will have to ignore the looks of disapproval from the greengrocer. A good lemon is a ripe one, and there are fewer about than you might imagine. They should be firm but not rock hard, and heavy for their size. The real hard whoppers invariably yield little juice. Those slightly softer, medium-sized and thin-skinned seem to be more generously endowed with juice, though less easy to grate.

Much of the joy of a lemon is in its zest, the aromatic yellow skin where most of the flavour is contained. Zest is a very appropriate word. Unfortunately, the average lemon has been plied with fungicides, insecticides and waxes to make it more appealing to the eye, which means that grating an unwashed lemon into your cake mix is tantamount to adding a teaspoon of chemicals too.

Lemons straight from the tree do not shine dazzlingly. They have a gentle hue to them. You can find untreated lemons in some major stores and, of course, health food and organic shops. But they are far from accessible to most of us, so my advice is to wash your lemons under running water, though avoid scrubbing them so hard you take off the top layer of zest.

Grating Lemons

Overzealous grating will lead to bitterness. What you want is the thin yellow top coat of the skin: it's where the best of the lemon's flavour lurks. The white layer beneath is mouth-puckeringly bitter. It's called the pith, and should be left on the fruit rather than stirred into the pudding. So go easy with the grater, and use the small holes.

Lemon Syllabub

All recipes for lemon syllabub include a statutory overnight marinating of lemon peel in brandy. This act, though simplicity in itself, may well be the reason for this delightful dessert's fall from grace. The quick, perhaps heretical, method below includes grating the lemon zest instead. Just the way they do in most restaurants.

FOR 4, WITH SECOND HELPINGS

1 lemon	75g / 3oz caster sugar
2 tablespoons brandy	300ml / ½ pint double cream
75ml / 3fl oz sweet sherry	

Grate the zest from the lemon on the fine side of the grater, taking care not to include the bitter white pith underneath. Put to one side. Cut the lemon in half and squeeze the juice into a large mixing bowl. Add the brandy and sherry. Stir in the sugar till pretty well dissolved.

Add the cream in a steady stream, electric whisk in one hand, cream in the other. Take care that you are not whisking too fast, in which case it will become buttery and grainy very suddenly. A hand whisk will give better control if you can bear it. When the cream leaves a soft trail from the whisk, and settles in drifts rather than peaks, it is ready. Stir in the grated zest. Spoon into glasses and chill for a few minutes.

Little Pots of Lemon Cream

If richness alone could be a measure of excellence then these pots of lemon cream would win hands down. To all but the most serious lemon dessert addicts their tart unctuousness may overwhelm.

FOR 2

4 tablespoons good lemon curd	2 tablespoons *crème fraîche*
2 tablespoons thick, Greek-style yoghurt	1 teaspoon finely grated lemon zest

Stir together the ingredients, then spoon into tiny glasses, *demi-tasse* coffee cups or even egg cups. Dot with a crystallised violet – a proper one, not one of those purple icing-sugar impostors – chill for 10 minutes and eat with a teaspoon.

CHEESES FOR SPRING

I quite often break off a lump of cheese, or slice it if that is more appropriate, to eat at the end of my meal. I have lost interest, and I never had very much, in the cellophane-wrapped specimens at the chilled counter. They all taste like soap to me. Even the mature ones are just sharp; they have no real depth of flavour. You can't beat a piece cut from a farmhouse cheese, properly made in the traditional manner. And preferably with unpasteurised milk. Fortunately, due to a growing band of passionate cheesemakers, we can buy fine cheese in delis, grocers and some supermarkets as well as in specialist cheese shops. Even some of the supermarkets are selling slender pieces of hand-made cheeses, though I find it is better to buy a large lump from a smaller shop. It always seems in better condition.

The British cheeses that were made last autumn and have been maturing ever since should be a joy to eat by now. In particular, crumbly creamy-white Caerphilly. Duckett's is a reliable name to look out for. Its slight tartness marries well with bland sweet pears if you can find any good ones at this time of year, and with Spanish quince cheese, the dark pink conserve sold by the block in some delis and cheese shops.

Other firm British cheese good to eat in March, April and May is Cheshire, especially Mrs Appleby's firm, orange-fleshed, unpasteur-ised one, and many of the Cheddars will make very fine eating now. A cheese specialist will guide you to a Cheddar that is right, but you can really only tell if it is the one for you by tasting it. If you go to a cheese shop they will probably have several Cheddars to choose from. Names to look out for are: Montgomery (a deeply flavoured, nutty cheese made from unpasteurised milk); Quickes, a milder cheese, and accessible through some supermarkets; and Keen's, a lovely, slightly grainy Cheddar.

Summer

4

cherries · **strawberries** · *raspberries* ·
other berries and currants · *peaches* ·
the *brûlée* · *melons* · **cheeses**

*F*ast food is somehow especially pertinent to summer. I will go to extreme lengths not to put the oven on of a warm summer evening. If I can be persuaded to cook at all it will be something of the minimum fuss maximum effect variety. Puddings too at this time of year must involve as little preparation and cooking as possible. At the very height of the season, with temperatures as high as they go, all I am really interested in is twenty new ways to serve a ripe melon.

An abundance of fine-flavoured fruit means that puddings can be prepared in minutes all summer long. The simpler the idea, the more pleasing the result – a glass of red berries topped up with Sauternes, a bowl of strawberries showered with mellow balsamic vinegar or cubes of refreshing melon scattered with shredded basil leaves.

After a generous plate of leafy salad, or perhaps some cold pasta dressed with olive oil and fresh young garlic, I want nothing more than a dish of perfectly ripe fruit. If something a little more substantial is required I may mix it with some cheese. Watermelon and Feta perhaps, or a great favourite of mine, goat's cheese and cherries. Whether your interests lie in a bowl of raspberries, warm from the sun, or a compote of raspberries and blueberries as rich as red velvet, fruit is the backbone of summer puddings.

CHERRIES

I said in *Real Fast Food* that cherries only inspire me when they are eaten from the stalk out of the greengrocer's brown paper bag. If I am to eat them at all they must have a little tartness to them, and be deep red or yellow and vermilion in colour. Sweet, black gobstopper varieties leave me cold.

Cherries and Chèvre
The second best way with cherries is to eat them with goat's cheese. Choose a soft, fresh *chèvre*. An ash-covered log is ideal. Slice it into rounds, about 1cm / ½ inch thick, and lay two or three on each plate. Drop a handful of ripe red and yellow cherries, stalks attached, over each one. Unless the *chèvre* is very soft I usually push a little of the cheese on to each cherry with my knife as I eat.

Hot Cherries with Calvados

One of the few hot summer puddings that are worth the trouble. Expect it to take a full 10 minutes of your time.

FOR 4

450g / 1lb cherries
25g / 1oz butter
50g / 2oz sugar
2 tablespoons Calvados or Cognac

Vanilla ice cream, *fromage frais* or thick, Greek-style yoghurt, to serve

Pull the stalks from the cherries. Melt the butter in a frying pan, add the sugar and the Calvados or Cognac and mix well over the heat. Throw in the cherries and toss them around gently in the bubbling mixture. Cook over a high heat till they start to caramelise. Lift the cherries from the pan with a draining spoon and divide between four warm plates. Add a dollop of ice cream, *fromage frais* or thick yoghurt at the side.

Strawberries see also pages 75–6, 98, 173, 178, 183–4

A bowl of ripe strawberries and cream, one of the fastest puddings there is. And yet it can be bettered so easily. Particularly if you keep the cream for raspberries, and sprinkle the strawberries with a little sugar and red wine instead. If cream it must be, then at least invest in some *crème fraîche*, whose slight sharpness will lift the flavour of the fruit, and whose unctuousness will contrast with the fruit's crunchy seeds.

There are probably over a hundred varieties of strawberry. Stafford Whiteaker's fascinating little book on strawberries mentions one and a half a dozen, Edward Bunyard's *Anatomy of Dessert* a good two dozen. Ken Muir, the strawberry specialist, stocks even more than that. But these are gardeners' strawberries, though there is no reason why a few plants cannot survive on a warm windowsill. Then you wouldn't even have to shop for them.

In the shops, however, we are hardly ever given a choice, even though many of their seasons overlap. The large chain stores that have recently put a great deal of effort into offering us old varieties of apples might do well to go to the same trouble over our famous and much loved berries. At the moment we know only if they are French, English or Californian. A fact that tells us little about the flavour.

Choosing strawberries is fraught with difficulties. Here are a few points which might help you to avoid disappointment.

* Check the bottom of the punnet to make sure it is dry. If it is stained with juice the berries at the bottom will be past it

* Buy your berries from a greengrocer you know, someone who is not likely to rip you off with punnets containing squashy fruit under a few good-looking berries

* Supermarket strawberries often have a hole in the top of the packaging; sniff the berries through it – if they are fragrant then they may well be good to eat

* Do not disregard berries from Spain or Israel, even out of season, as much work has gone into making the fruit taste good. The early Spanish strawberries are, to my mind, some of the best we ever get

* A little whiteness around the top is not always a bad sign. Such berries will respond to a short time in a warm room, or can be perked up with balsamic vinegar, see pages 149–50

* I am sorry, but whoppers labelled 'Californian' are rarely worth the money; in fact, they are as bad as the imports from Holland. Plump and red to look at, utterly tasteless to eat

* I find the best way to perk up slightly underripe strawberries or those short on flavour is to slice them in half and place them in a bowl with a sprinkling of sugar. Set aside in a covered bowl for half an hour before eating

Strawberries and Cream

I was brought up on strawberries and evaporated milk. The thought of which now makes me shudder. The boiled taste of the thin cream is not that far removed from that which now passes as double cream. Avoid at all costs anything labelled UHT. It has been heated to such an ultra-high temperature that its flavour has gone too. It also has a grey-white tinge to it. Look out instead for cream from small dairies. You must expect to pay more for it. But it is worth it.

Yellow cream from Jersey cows is the best, though not as suitable as the piquant French style *crème fraîche*. It is much easier to find nowadays; even my small grocer's shop stocks Loseley, which is as good a make as you will find. Much other cream is pale and thin. And tasteless. If it was unpasteurised I am sure its flavour would be even better. But bureaucrats who have no tastebuds and hysterical do-gooders have put paid to such treats.

Strawberries in Beaujolais

Slice washed strawberries into a china bowl. Sprinkle with Beaujolais, or some other light, fruity red wine. Set aside in a cool place for as long as you can. Half an hour should just about do it.

Strawberries with Black Pepper

The instructions 'strawberries taste good with a grinding of black pepper' is hardly news, but a little more detail is needed if the dish is to be a success.

The pepper *must*, absolutely *must*, be from freshly ground black peppercorns. It should be finely ground but far from dust, and it should be done very, very sparingly.

The point is to heighten the natural flavour of the berry without noticeably adding any pepperiness.

Strawberries with Basil

If I want a little pepperiness with my strawberries I would rather add basil, the herb whose aromatic leaves have a similar but more subtle effect.

FOR 2
225g / 8oz strawberries
a little lemon juice
1 tablespoon finely shredded basil leaves

Remove the stalks from the strawberries and cut each fruit in half. Sprinkle with lemon juice, then scatter over the shredded basil leaves. Toss the fruit very gently with a large spoon. Leave for 15 or 20 minutes before eating at room temperature.

Strawberries with Passion Fruit

Cut a heavy, wrinkled passion fruit in half. Squeeze its orange juice and little black seeds with their golden halo over a bowl of halved and hulled strawberries. Cover with a plate and leave for 15 minutes. Lift the lid, inhale the wonderful fragrance and eat, crunching the little seeds with the soft fruit.

Strawberries with Mint and Orange

Mint has a very pronounced, clean flavour. You won't need much of it to perk up your bowl of berries. Squeeze a generous amount of orange juice over a bowl of hulled berries. You will need the juice of two large oranges per 450g / 1lb of strawberries. Snip some tiny, sweet mint leaves into little bits, then stir them gently into the fruit and juice. Two or three sprigs of the herb is all you will need for a pound or so of the berries.

And with Cassis

Cassis, the intensely fruity blackcurrant liqueur, flatters rather than bullies a bowl of berries.

450g / 1lb strawberries, hulled
2 tablespoons Cassis
thick, Greek-style yoghurt, to serve

Cut the berries in half, sprinkle them with the Cassis and set aside at room temperature for 15 minutes. Eat with spoonfuls of thick yoghurt.

And with Balsamic Vinegar

Marcella Hazan, the doyenne of Italian cookery writers whose thoroughly researched and tested recipes put most others to shame, is probably responsible for bringing this bizarre-sounding idea to our attention. It has a heavenly fragrance, deeply sweet and rich, and is my favourite way of all to eat strawberries.

The point she makes in her book, *Marcella's Kitchen*, is that the vinegar is especially good for perking up strawberries that are not yet ripe. 'As though they had been penetrated by the most ardent of summer suns' is how she describes the result of macerating unripe berries in the mellow brown liquid.

Remove the leaves and stalks, cut large berries in half and put them in a bowl. Add a little sugar, perhaps 2 tablespoons per 450g / 1lb of fruit. Set aside for 25 minutes or so (an hour would be better), until the strawberries have released some of their juices to form a light syrup with the sugar. Add the balsamic vinegar. A tablespoon to the pound. Or 1 tablespoon to 450g as they say nowadays.

And with Lime Juice

Much better than lemon or orange I think. Cut a lime in half and squeeze its juice over the fruit. Eat immediately.

Strawberries with Rose Petal Cream

A straightforward enough recipe from Joyce Molyneux's old restaurant, The Carved Angel at Dartmouth in Devon. The soft rose fragrance is delightful with the ripe fruit. Claret coloured, deeply perfumed, old-fashioned roses are the ones for this. Make sure you know that they haven't been sprayed with insecticide. You can either layer the cream and fruit in glasses as they did at the restaurant, or serve it on a plate, surrounding a pile of ripe berries. Either way, this fragrant dessert is a doddle.

FOR 4–6

1 fragrant, dark red rose	lemon juice
150ml / ¼ pint single cream	150ml / ¼ pint double cream
1 tablespoon caster sugar	450g / 1lb strawberries

Separate the rose petals. Whizz them with the single cream, sugar and a dash of lemon juice in a blender. Mix with the double cream and whisk lightly. Hull the strawberries and halve if large. Layer with the rose petal cream in a single bowl or in individual glasses.

Strawberry Fool

Lumpy with chunks of fruit and sharpened by *fromage frais*, a fool far better than the toothpaste-like commercial ones.

FOR 2

225g / 8oz strawberries, hulled
225g / 8oz *fromage frais*
100ml / 4fl oz *crème fraîche* or thick double cream

Crush the berries in a pudding basin with a fork. Fold in the *fromage frais* and the *crème fraîche* or cream, slowly but thoroughly. Spoon into glasses or small pots and chill before serving – leave it for as long as possible. An almond biscuit or shortbread would make a flattering accompaniment.

Strawberries with Syllabub Sauce

FOR 4

100g / 4oz caster sugar
300ml / ½ pint double cream
4 tablespoons Marsala or
    medium dry sherry
450g / 1lb strawberries

1 teaspoon vanilla extract (not
    essence)
juice and finely grated zest of
    1 orange

Put the sugar, cream, Marsala or sherry, extract, juice and zest in a mixing bowl. Beat with an electric whisk till thick and creamy, but not actually stiff. Remove the stalks and leaves from the strawberries; cut the fruit into quarters. Put them in the bottom of four large balloon wineglasses or small china bowls.

Spoon the syllabub mixture over the strawberries. Refrigerate till needed, but for at least 20 minutes if you can.

RASPBERRIES *see also pages 52, 127, 169–70, 171, 177–8*

Lightly crushed against the side of the bowl raspberries reveal a fragrance that, combined with a little warmth from the sun, is positively intoxicating.

The deeper red the fruit, the more luscious it will be to eat. Pale pink raspberries hold few pleasures. Choose unblemished, dark-coloured fruits. Check them for flavour by carefully sniffing them; if their fragrance is obvious they will probably be good. Some of the French raspberries appearing early in the season smell almost alcoholic. As if someone has spilled *framboise* over them.

Much as I love raspberries I will not confine them to being eaten with nothing but cream, perfection though such simplicity can be. Raspberries and their sister berries have enough clout that they can be used in pastries, fruit salads, compotes and trifles. Raspberries, unlike strawberries, were made for cream. They make the finest of syllabubs and finish a close second to gooseberries in the fools' race.

Berries on a Leaf

An absurdly easy and beautiful presentation. It will impress even those used to the most elaborate of puddings.

Cover a plain white plate with raspberry or rose leaves, then carefully pile, a handful at a time, the velvet berries as high as you can. Serve a jug of cream and caster sugar on the side.

Raspberries in Gewürztraminer

Drop a handful of the berries into a glass of chilled sweetish wine. Gewürztraminer would suit, though others spring to mind like Moscatel or Beaumes de Venise.

Raspberries with Pistachios

Tip the berries into a bowl. Shell the pistachios (you will need a small handful of shelled nuts for each punnet of berries) then chop them coarsely with a knife. Scatter them over the fruit.

Raspberries with Almonds

FOR 4

225g / 8oz raspberries	50g / 2oz cake crumbs – a
50g / 2oz sugar	crumbled trifle sponge would
50g / 2oz almonds, very finely	be fine
chopped	6 tablespoons double cream

Put the berries into a small saucepan with the sugar and cook till the juices leak from the fruit and the sugar has dissolved, about 3 minutes over medium heat.

Fold the finely chopped nuts and the cake crumbs into the fruit and its juice, then spoon them into small glasses. Chill in the refrigerator, then pour the cream over the top. Eat at once.

Raspberries and Cream

The finest of all marriages, dark, blood-red raspberries and rich yellow cream. Offer *crème fraîche* for its piquancy, and a bowl of sugar for its pleasant crystalline grittiness as much as its sweetness.

Raspberry Fool

FOR 4

225g / 8oz raspberries
1 teaspoon lemon juice
225ml / 8fl oz double cream, softly whipped

Whizz the raspberries in the food processor till smooth. Add the lemon juice, then fold in the softly whipped cream. Serve in glasses with crisp biscuits.

Another Raspberry Fool

FOR 4

225g / 8oz raspberries
150ml / ¼ pint double cream
100ml / 4fl oz thick, Greek-style yoghurt

Whizz half the berries till smooth. Whip the cream until it forms soft peaks, stir in the yoghurt and then the puréed berries. Fold in the reserved whole berries and spoon between four glasses.

Iced Raspberry Fool

Whizz, stir, whip, fold, freeze.

FOR 4

450g / 1lb raspberries
50g / 2oz sugar
200ml / 7fl oz double cream

Whizz the raspberries in a food processor.
Stir in the sugar.
Whip the cream till it forms soft peaks.
Gently fold the fruit purée into the cream.
Tip into bowl and freeze for 2 hours.

Raspberry Syllabub

Making this syllabub was a daily task during the summer and autumn when I once worked in the kitchens of a castle turned restaurant. It was an afternoon job, done when all was peaceful. Sometimes we would run out and I would have to whip one up quickly in the middle of a very busy service. It has remained one of my favourite real fast puddings ever since.

FOR 4

225g / 8oz raspberries	1 tablespoon *framboise* or
4 tablespoons caster sugar	rosewater
225ml / 8fl oz double cream	150ml / ¼ pint sweet white wine

Put half of the raspberries into a large bowl and crush them gently against the side with a metal spoon. They will bleed a little. Sprinkle with the sugar and the *framboise* or rosewater. Beat the cream with an electric or hand whisk until it starts to thicken. It should be thick and unctuous and will slowly fall from the spoon. It must not be what you might call 'whipped'. Slowly beat the wine into the cream, which must stand in drifts rather than peaks.

Carefully add the cream to the macerating fruit, folding them slowly together with a metal spoon. Throw in the remaining raspberries. Serve in glasses, perhaps with little almond biscuits, like the ones the German biscuit manufacturers are so good at.

Little Raspberry Soufflés

FOR 4

a little butter and sugar	1 teaspoon *framboise*, Kirsch or
350g / 12oz raspberries	neither
75g / 3oz caster sugar	3 egg whites
	icing sugar, to dust

Rub a little butter round the inside of four small ovenproof moulds.

They can be those white china ramekins if you have them, or even cups, though not thin porcelain ones. Sprinkle a little sugar over the butter, then turn the dishes upside down and shake off the surplus.

Whizz the raspberries in the processor to form a purée. Add half of the sugar. You can sieve the mixture at this point if you hate raspberry pips. I rather like the mild crunchiness of the little things amid the general smoothness. Add the *framboise* or Kirsch.

Whisk the egg whites till stiff; they should stand in peaks. Add the remaining sugar with a metal spoon using a gentle folding motion. Stir a little of the fruit purée into the egg whites, mix gently, then fold the egg whites into the fruit purée. Do this with a large metal spoon as before, gently bringing the mixture up from the bottom and over the egg whites till they are all mixed.

Fill the little dishes or cups with the raspberry mixture. Bake in a preheated oven, 180°C/350°F (gas mark 5), until puffed and slightly cracked, about 12 minutes. Dust with a little icing sugar if you wish. Serve immediately.

Almond Raspberry Shortcake

The method looks long here, but it is unlikely to take you more than half an hour or so. It takes five minutes to make the pastry and ten to rest it, fifteen or so to cook it and ten to cool and decorate it. Hardly an evening's work.

FOR 4

100g / 4oz plain flour
2 tablespoons ground almonds
pinch of salt
75g / 3oz butter
50g / 2oz caster sugar

1 egg, separated
caster sugar
raspberries
double cream

Put the flour and almonds into the food processor with the salt. Add the butter cut into little chunks and whizz for a few seconds till you have what looks like breadcrumbs.

Add the sugar. Whizz once. Add the yolk of the egg and whizz slowly till the whole lot comes together in a big lump. Stop. Turn the dough out on to a baking sheet. You won't need to butter it if it's an old one. Press the dough out into a disc about 17.5cm / 7 inches in diameter. You can crimp the edges prettily if you wish. I tend not to.

Prick with a fork and rest the pastry in the fridge for 10 minutes. You will probably have to take everything else out to get the tray in. Preheat the oven to 200°C/400°F (gas mark 6). Bake the almond pastry till very pale gold in colour, no darker than a piece of short-bread, for about 15 minutes. Beat the egg white briefly with a fork and brush a little of it over the pastry. Sprinkle it with a bit of caster sugar. Return it to the oven for 3 or 4 minutes.

Remove from the oven. Lift the disc carefully on to a cooling rack, or the rack from the grill pan, with the aid of a long, thin spatula. The perforated fish slice will do. While it is cooling whip the cream into soft peaks.

To assemble, put the almond pastry on to a large plate. Pile the cream in soft waves over the top. Don't fuss about this too much. Place the raspberries on top and eat immediately.

Warmed Raspberries

Tip the raspberries into an ovenproof dish. Sprinkle over a little sugar and leave them in a very low oven, 150°C/300°F (gas mark 2), for 25 minutes or so. They will have produced copious red juice. Add just a touch, and I mean just a touch, of Cassis or Kirsch or, of course, *framboise*. The rich wine-red juices, now heady with raspberries and liqueur, are the point of the thing. Serve in pretty glasses, still warm, with elegant biscuits from a posh packet.

OTHER BERRIES AND CURRANTS

I often use a mixture of berries and currants in summer desserts (though I happily use frozen ones in the winter). By a mixture, I mean two or three from a list of purple, black, red and blue berries: raspberries; tayberries; loganberries and mulberries; red, white and blackcurrants; blueberries and blackberries. I rarely include straw-berries as they become so nasty with the application of heat. I am not sure that there is a right combination of subtle and strident fruits, and often just throw in whatever is to hand. Watch the blackcurrants, though, as they can be overpowering in quantity, especially when up against some of the more unusual red berries.

A Plate of Claret, Purple and Blue Berries

Tip dusty-blue blueberries, black and dark red blackberries and glis-tening loganberries and redcurrants from their punnets on to a platter. Eaten by candlelight, the berries will sparkle and intrigue, like costume jewellery.

An Incomplete Guide to the Less Common Berries

Mulberries
I am quite crazy about these luscious, fragile fruits. Too soft to send to market in quantity, they are a delicacy among berries, and lucky are those who live within picking distance of a mulberry tree. The purple-crimson fruits hide behind the tree's large leaves then drop in brilliant splodges all around the roots. Eat them for what they are, a truly rare treat, with a small amount of single cream.

Blueberries　　see also page 113
A beautiful dusty-blue colour, round with a slightly flattened top and bottom. Perfect for the short-of-time, as there is no need to top and

tail. Interesting enough when raw, its flavour is both sharp and bland, but sensational when cooked. American originally, but now grown in Dorset and Hampshire. One of the world's great berries.

Bilberries
A rare treat found growing wild in Scotland and Yorkshire. Occasionally makes the shops but the somewhat similar-tasting blueberry has stolen much of its glory. Smooth-skinned and purply-black in colour.

Redcurrants and Whitecurrants   see also page 183
A favourite fruit of mine – it is their acidity that appeals; at last these diminutive jewel-like fruits are becoming more popular. Generally around during June, July and August, they are very much a sign that high summer has arrived. Apart from their tartness, which no doubt puts off those for whom sweetness is all, they are annoying to prepare. Having picked them for pocket money as a child I learned to strip them from their delicate stems in seconds. Just hold each sprig in one hand and quickly pull at the berries using all the fingers of your free hand. Picking each fruit individually will take an age.

Blackcurrants   see also pages 98–9, 129
The point of the blackcurrant is the sublime, deeply coloured and flavoured juices that appear when it is cooked. Apply a little heat and each round, black sphere splits its skin to reveal rich purple juices of great intensity. Only the brave will fail to add sugar, generally 2 tablespoons of caster to the half-pound of berries. A wonderfully strident flavour to perk up crumbles, ices and poached pears. Commercially they are used to produce Cassis, the purple liqueur which forms the heart of a kir.

Tayberries
A cross between a raspberry and a blackberry, though the flavour is distinctly more like the latter. Somehow less exciting than its parents, though juicy enough to eat on its own with just a little cream.

Fraises des bois   *see also pages 52, 184*

The tiniest of the berries, but with a pure flavour reminiscent of a cross between a modern strawberry and vanilla. Its copious little seeds provide a welcome crunchiness that has virtually been bred out of the larger strawberries. I see them rarely in anything but the most elite of food shops, and at odd times of the year, depending on where they are grown. The best, of course, are those you find in the wild, twinkling in the hedgerows like little red and white stars.

Loganberries   *see also page 171*

This longer, softer version of the raspberry is a successful result of a blackberry / raspberry cross. First found in California, it has all the joys of a raspberry with the benefit of a little more acidity. Expect to find them in the shops during July and August.

Boysenberries

One of the earliest of the berry family, appearing in early summer, usually imported from New Zealand, and tasting like a tart blackberry. Something of a hybrid experiment, it has a dubious parentage of raspberries, blackberries and strawberries. Its lack of identity is a mixed blessing, to my mind.

Cheat's Summer Pudding

Proper summer pudding should be weighted and left overnight for the juices from the raspberries, red and blackcurrants to soak through the bread. But the different flavours of the berries have already been married in the cooking pot and anyone can soak bread in purple-black juice. So here is a quick version that has much the same flavour, and the same soggy, fruity bread. The only count it fails on is that it just won't stand up. So? Serve it from the bowl, with cream.

175g / 6oz blackcurrants
175g / 6oz redcurrants
175g / 6oz raspberries

75g / 3oz caster sugar
4 slices of white bread

Remove the stalks from the currants. Put the fruit and sugar in a stainless steel saucepan with 3 tablespoons of water. Bring to the boil, then cook gently till the currants burst their skins and form a rich, purple-red syrup. This usually takes about 5–7 minutes.

Cut the crusts from the bread and cut it into small triangles, about four from each slice. Place a few of them in the bottom of a 23cm / 9 inch shallow china dish and cover with some of the warm fruit. Make another layer of bread and another of fruit. Continue till all the bread and fruit are used up. It would be a good idea to finish with a layer of bread if you can. Spoon the warm juice over the bread, pressing gently down with the back of a spoon until the bread is completely soaked.

Set aside for as much time as you have. Fifteen minutes should do it. Don't attempt to turn it out of the dish. Spoon into bowls and eat with cream.

Berries in Beaumes de Venise

FOR 4

450g / 1lb blueberries, raspberries and strawberries
½ bottle of Beaumes de Venise, chilled

Put the berries, cut in half if large, into wineglasses. Top up with the cold Beaumes de Venise and serve immediately.

Warm Red Fruit Compote

A 10-minute hot pudding, unless the currants have their stalks on. In which case it will take a little longer. Serve with a jug of cream, to swirl into the glorious purple-red juices.

225g / 8oz redcurrents   450g / 1lb raspberries,
100g / 4oz blackcurrants   loganberries or tayberries
4 tablespoons sugar

Put the currants, having first removed their stalks, into a stainless steel saucepan with 2 tablespoons of water and the sugar. Bring slowly to the boil. When the currants start to burst and flood the pan with colour, then tip in the raspberries, loganberries or whatever. Simmer for 2 minutes, no longer, and serve them warm, in a white china dish.

Red and Whitecurrants with Fromage Frais

Either of the currants is very enjoyable eaten in this way. Unmould some *fromage frais* on to a plate. Surround it with little sprigs of currants, red and white. Sit in the shade spreading the fresh, white cheese on to tiny, crisp water biscuits, then scatter over a few red or whitecurrants. Utter bliss.

Six Uses for a Red Fruit Compote

* Serve the compote warm, with shop-bought meringues and double cream

* Use the compote as an accompaniment for a sponge cake. Buy a good one from a proper patisserie or cake shop, and spoon a little compote around each slice

* Pour the hot fruit and their juices over vanilla ice cream, watching the ice cream melt into the hot purple syrup

* Stir some of the juices into a tub of thick natural yoghurt. Eat it straight from the tub

* Stir the compote into a bowl of stewed apples

* Use the fruit as the filling for crêpes (see page 101–2), then spoon the juices round the plate

Gooseberries   see also page 59–60

I suspect that gooseberries fall into the same category as liver, rhubarb, kidneys and mackerel. There are those who love them and those who cannot stand them, but few who have no strong feelings either way. For the record, I rank them as one of the finest fruits we grow. I would rather have a bowl of hot baked gooseberries with cold, sharp *crème fraîche* than a bowl of strawberries and cream any day.

I have known some to make more fuss about topping-and-tailing gooseberries than is really justified. It takes barely 2 minutes to stalk and flower a pound of goosegogs – I have timed it. Unless the flowers are very large and the stalk singularly tough, I am not so sure they always need it anyway. Whatever, you can have them rinsed and prepared in less than 5 minutes. And they take barely 15 to cook.

Grilled Gooseberries with Saffron and Honey

Cream and gooseberries is a marriage made in heaven. In this alternative summer dessert the gooseberries are served hot with cold double cream or *crème fraîche*, which mingles with the buttery honey and saffron-scented gooseberry juices.

FOR 2

450g / 1lb gooseberries	pinch of saffron stamens
butter	caster sugar
2 tablespoons runny honey	cream of *crème fraîche*, to serve

Rinse the fruit in a colander under the cold tap, then top and tail them. Butter a 20cm / 8 inch baking dish. Be generous. Throw in the goosegogs, the honey and saffron and stir. Place in a preheated oven, 180°C/350°F (gas mark 4), for 15 minutes till they are plump and about to burst.

Remove the dish from the oven and turn on the grill. Sprinkle with caster sugar, then grill till caramelised and golden on top. Serve warm, with double cream or *crème fraîche*, making the most of the cooking juices.

Whitecurrants in Moscatel

Several of the major stores now stock a sparkling Moscatel. It is to my mind a frivolous, light, slightly fizzy wine perfectly suited to drinking out of doors.

A favourite pudding of mine last summer involved a handful of glistening whitecurrants dropped unceremoniously into a wineglass and topped up with chilled sparkling Moscatel.

Redcurrants and Sauternes

Pick the scarlet currants from their fragile stems. Pile them into a glass bowl and sprinkle with caster sugar and a little very golden, very sweet Sauternes.

PEACHES *see also pages 177–8, 184*

The perfect fast pudding – a plate of magnificently ripe, crimson-blushed peaches, fragrant from a foot away and wonderfully juicy to eat. It is quite possible too; I have found peaches in perfect condition from May to October in the large chain stores and for a slightly shorter season at the greengrocer's, much more easily than was the case a few years ago.

Even the white peach, once so difficult to find, now makes more than a fleeting appearance in big-name supermarkets. Its flesh is creamy white tinged with vermilion, its scent (to this nose anyway) a cross between roses and raspberries.

A ripe peach is a perfumed one. To test for ripeness, sniff rather than squeeze. The aroma should be sweet. Only the very ripest will require a refrigerator, and will be difficult to get home unbruised. Perhaps better to buy half a dozen at once and ripen them yourself over a few days, in a brown paper bag. Bring them to room temperature before you eat, though, as it is then that their fragrance is at its height.

I have no doubt that the French and Italian peaches have the best flavour. Those from further afield rarely match the sublime sweet juiciness of fruit from closer to home. I have never bought a peach out of season (November to April) that was worth the money. The peach is the perfect partner for almonds and anything made from them, thick creams with a bite to them, and soft cheeses, even blue ones. Dropped into a glass of not too sweet, very cold wine, it makes one of the best fast desserts I know of.

Nectarines do not hold the same magic for me. I miss the fuzzy skin of the peach, and rarely find the nectarine, its bald cousin, as sexy to eat. But many prefer the nectarine whose scarlet skin is so tempting, and the fruits are, of course, quite interchangeable in the ideas that follow. Late June, July and August are the best months for these fruits, and their abundance and reasonable price allow one to exploit their juice and flavour all summer long.

Stripey Cheese and Blushing Fruit

There is a smart hybrid cheese that is made up of layers of Dolcelatte and Mascarpone, the Italian blue and soft creamy cheeses. It looks too snazzy to be good. In a narrow-minded, elitist sort of way, I ignored it for some time. (I lost out on years of peanut butter and jam sandwiches that way too.)

I have become very fond of splitting ripe peaches in half, removing the stones, then stuffing the hollows with blobs of this striped cheese. It is especially good if the cheese is colder than you would usually serve it, and if the peaches are lusciously, dribblingly ripe.

Peaches with Orange Blossom Honey

You can enlist any of the flower honeys; a mixed one will do fine but use lavender or orange blossom if you can. Their character seems to come out when warmed under the grill.

FOR 4

4 tablespoons runny honey   **2 ripe peaches**
juice of 1 lemon   **4 teaspoons butter**

Mix the honey with the lemon juice in a small bowl. Cut the peaches in half and remove the stones. Place the fruit, flat side up, in a shallow baking dish.

Dot a teaspoon of butter in the hollow of each peach, spoon the lemon and honey mixture over the fruit and place under a preheated medium-hot grill. The peaches are done when the honey starts to bubble and they turn golden brown in patches, about 5–7 minutes.

Grilled Amaretti *Peaches*

Follow the previous recipe, but forget the butter. Before you spoon over the honey and lemon, stuff the peach halves with the following mixture:

FOR 4

50g / 2oz Ricotta cheese
6 *amaretti* biscuits, crushed in their papers or in a paper bag with a rolling pin

Spoon over the honey and lemon and place under the preheated grill until the almond cheese filling begins to brown, about 5–7 minutes. Serve hot, spooning the syrup from the baking dish over the peaches.

Poached Peaches with Grand Marnier

FOR 2

4 ripe peaches, not too large
100g / 4oz sugar
225ml / 8fl oz water

1 vanilla pod
4 slices of orange
2 tablespoons Grand Marnier

Halve the peaches and remove the stones. Put the sugar, water, vanilla and orange slices, but not the liqueur, in a pan large enough to hold the fruit in one layer. Bring to the boil and turn down to a simmer. Add the fruit and poach it gently. The syrup should just cover the peaches; if it doesn't then make a little more.

After 5–10 minutes the peaches, depending on their ripeness, will be tender and soaked with the vanilla and orange syrup. Remove from the heat. Place the peaches in a serving dish, then spoon over the syrup. Add the Grand Marnier and leave to cool a little before eating.

Peach Melba

People scoff at peach Melbas. And well they might, there is something deeply tacky about such things. But a peach Melba can be a thing of joy. If you can excuse its garish orange, pink and white, it can taste quite superb. But there are rules.

* The peach must be ripe. It must never have seen a tin

* The peach should be poached lightly in vanilla-scented syrup

* The sauce should be made from puréed raspberries. There is no reason why they shouldn't have been frozen at some point

* The ice cream should be vanilla, not Neapolitan, and should be of the very best quality. None of your 'soft scoop Cornish'

* It should really be called *Pêches Melba*

FOR 4

4 ripe peaches
2 tablespoons caster sugar
1 vanilla pod

225g / 8oz raspberries
very good vanilla ice cream

Place the whole peaches in a saucepan with just enough water to cover them. Throw in the sugar and the vanilla pod. Bring to the boil and poach them in simmering water for 8–10 minutes. Remove with a slotted spoon. The peaches are ready when their skins peel off easily. Do this carefully so as not to damage the fruit. Cut each one in half and gently ease out the stone. Place the peach halves in a cool place.

Get four glass bowls as cold as you can. Whizz the raspberries in the food processor until they are puréed (you can sieve them at this point to remove the pips if you wish). Taste the purée. You may feel it needs a little sugar. I can't honestly say I have ever added any to a raspberry purée, but if you want a sweeter result now is the time to get the icing sugar out.

Place a large, solid ball of ice cream in each chilled dish. Place two halves of peach each side of the ice cream, then drizzle over some of the raspberry purée.

The Cream Question

There are some who say that a peach Melba is not a peach Melba unless it has whipped cream on it. No doubt that is what old Escoffier, the Savoy's chef, meant when he produced the pudding to honour Dame Nellie Melba. I insist that it is better without. But you may well disagree. Add a dollop of double cream if you wish, whipped quite stiff with a little vanilla extract.

But then if you are going to add a swirl of whipped cream, you might as well stick a cherry on top as well.

Marzipan Peaches

Heat the grill. Cut ripe peaches in half and remove the stones. Put a lump of almond paste in the hollow of each peach half. Sprinkle with rosewater and grill till the almond paste melts and turns golden. About 7–8 minutes. Eat warm.

Hot Peaches with Mascarpone and Pine Nuts

FOR 2

4 ripe peaches
4 tablespoons Mascarpone cheese
2 tablespoons pine nuts

Cut the peaches in half and remove the stones. Put the peaches in a shallow ovenproof dish, flat side up. Dot half a tablespoon of Mascarpone in the hollow of each peach. Scatter pine nuts over the cheese and place under a preheated hot grill till the cheese has melted and the pine nuts are golden.

Peaches with Brioche

My local chain store has started selling rather good brioche. It is a little 'cakey', but then Islington isn't Paris. I like eating the rich, yellow bread with a whole ripe peach. It is more of a snack than a dessert, but the two match up quite well. A bit like figs and *ciabatta* or pears and Bath Olivers.

Peaches with Raspberry Sauce

Pour boiling water over ripe peaches. Leave for 5 minutes, then carefully remove them from the water. Peel away the skins; they should lift off easily. Put a whole peach in the centre of each plate.

Whizz raspberries, fresh or frozen ones, in the blender or food processor with a few drops of Kirsch or some other compatible alcohol, and reduce to a purée. I think you had better sieve it to remove the little seeds. You might add a little lemon juice if you think about it. Pour the purée around the peaches and serve slightly chilled. The ubiquitous mint leaf, so beloved of young chefs, would actually serve some purpose here. Though it would be better chopped up and scattered over the dish.

You will probably need to eat this with a fork and a spoon. Otherwise the peach is likely to go slithering off the plate like a bar of wet soap.

Peaches with Port

I learned to like port on a fact-finding trip to Portugal. My hosts were one of the old port families whose *quintas* line the banks of the Douro, and I was plied with the stuff for my entire stay. (And for a good while afterwards.) It was the light white port that got to me; mixed with tonic and mint leaves it made a very pleasant early evening drink by the pool. After a little while the bottles started to mount up and, when the weather turned cooler, I started using it in other ways. This was by far the most successful, and I think worth repeating.

FOR 2
2 peaches, ripe and juicy
2 tablespoons white port
a little sugar

Slice the peaches into a bowl. Discard the stones. Upend the measure of port over them, then sprinkle with a little sugar. You might like the taste of the peaches without any sweetener, so try them first. Set aside for 20 minutes.

A Plate of White Peaches and Red Berries

A dessert plate for the end of a high summer meal. Arrange heavily perfumed white peaches on a pretty plate with a handful of fresh almonds, shelled but not skinned, and a little pile of deep red loganberries or raspberries.

Hot Peaches with Redcurrant Jelly

I suggest you buy some decent redcurrant jelly for this, so that the sauce tastes of fruit rather than sugar. Some of the French brands are good, and so are one or two of the smaller British ones.

FOR 2
350g / 12oz redcurrant jelly
4 ripe peaches

Melt the jelly in a small saucepan; if it is a good one it won't be too thick, but you may need to add a little water to achieve a smooth, slightly runny sauce. Cut the peaches in half, remove the stones and warm the peaches in the redcurrant sauce. Serve warm.

* Rose petal jam, from Middle Eastern grocers or posh food emporiums, is delightful used in this way

* So is quince jam, if you can find a brand that is quite soft and melts easily. Some of them are quite stiff

* If there is any left over, it will be just as good tomorrow. Especially if left in the cool rather than in the fridge

APRICOTS *see also page 58*

Apricots have a subtle, annoyingly elusive flavour and a fluffy texture. I am sure this is not how they should be. But it is increasingly how I find them. Lucky people who have eaten them straight from the tree assure me that they have a blushing, peach-like flesh and, when perfectly ripe, are blessed with a deep, sweet flavour.

I buy them, hoping each time they will be as good as I gather they can be. But I am invariably disappointed. I will not assume that you have any more luck when shopping than I do. The few ideas here are not for fools and mousses where the elusive flavour is smothered with bland ingredients, but instead the fruit is matched with something that teases out its shy flavour. Sharp creams, sweet muscat wines, aniseedy fennel and, in one case, the application of a little heat and sugar.

Grilled Apricots with Mascarpone

Golden apricots with a glistening sugary top.

FOR 2
6 ripe apricots
75g / 3oz / 12 teaspoons Mascarpone cheese
4 tablespoons caster sugar

Heat the grill. It needs to be really hot for this. Halve and stone the apricots and put them, hollow side up, in a heatproof dish. Place dollops of Mascarpone in the hollows. Sprinkle with half of the sugar and place the dish under the hot grill. Cook for 4 minutes, remove from the heat, sprinkle over the remaining sugar. Grill once more, till the fruit is tender with a crisp crust. Eat warm.

* Peaches work in this recipe too, as of course do nectarines. But I have also had success with dark red plums

Apricots Stuffed with Ricotta and Fennel

Apricots respond to any piquant cheese or cream. I perk up the overly subtle flavour of apricots with *crème fraîche*, thick yoghurt and, increasingly, Ricotta cheese. Sometimes I mix them; Ricotta or cottage cheese with yoghurt is a favourite. Surprisingly, some of the blue cheeses, such as salty and expensive Roquefort or less salty and less expensive Gorgonzola, make instant stuffings for apricots or peaches.

FOR 4

12 ripe apricots
100g / 4oz Ricotta cheese
150ml / ¼ pint thick,
   Greek-style yoghurt

2 tablespoons chopped fennel
   and its fronds

Cut the apricots in half just enough to pull out the stone. Try to keep the fruit intact at one point, which is easy enough to do if you follow the natural split in the fruit with your thumb. Set the fruit down on a plate. Mix the cheese and yoghurt, then stir in the fennel.

Spoon the fennel cheese mixture into the open apricots. A little sprig of green fennel frond in each fruit would be a nice touch if you can be bothered.

Apricots with Beaumes de Venise

Useful stuff, this sticky wine. The muscat tones of Beaumes de Venise are one way of making apricots laugh a little louder. Slice the ripe fruit, quarters will do, and drop the pieces into glasses of the chilled, sweet golden wine.

Apricots with Strawberry and Orange Sauce

Cut several ripe apricots in half. Remove the stones and place the fruit in a dish large enough to take them in a single layer. Butt them up closely with their hollows facing up. Whizz ripe strawberries in the food processor, add the juice of an orange and a little of its grated zest. Spoon the purée over the fruit. Leave for a little while before serving.

Warm Apricot Tarts

Crisp thin pastry. Juicy fruit.

FOR 2, GENEROUSLY
225g / 8oz ready-made puff pastry
8 ripe apricots
caster sugar

Roll out the pastry to a thickness of 3mm / ⅛ inch, which is thinner than you would normally expect. Cut two 15cm / 6 inch rounds of pastry and place on a baking sheet or wooden board. Chill in the fridge for 15 minutes.

Preheat the oven to 220°C/425°F (gas mark 7). Place an empty baking sheet in the oven. Bring a kettle of water to the boil. Place the apricots in a heatproof bowl and pour over the water. Leave for 1 minute, then remove with a slotted spoon.

Cut the apricots in half, peeling away the downy skin as you go. Remove the stones. Place the apricot halves, flat side down, on the rounds of chilled pastry and dust with a little caster sugar.

Transfer each one, using a fish slice or some such implement, to the hot baking sheet. The heat will help the pastry to crisp nicely. Bake for 10 minutes until puffed, crisp and golden. Eat while warm.

THE *BRÛLÉE*

Fruit, cream and sugar are combined in this glorious dessert, which no matter how extravagant its ingredients and indulgent its nature remains eternally popular. Its popularity rests no doubt on the mixture of textures between ripe fruit, thick, rich cream and crackling caramel crust.

In essence easy, the method is actually beset with little pitfalls, which can leave you with a sloppy mess resembling fruit soup.

The Cream
A stiff *crème fraîche* is my first choice, as it has something to offer in the way of flavour as well as voluptuousness. A sharp double cream would be my second. The cream should have flavour to it; a good quality double cream has more point to it than sheer unctuousness. Flat-tasting UHT creams provide creaminess but little else. Whipping cream, because of its low butterfat content, tends to 'fall' when the boiling caramel is poured over, and weeps if left for more than a few minutes before eating. Yoghurt is more successful than you might think, though it is prone to tantrums. Occasionally it curdles horribly when under the grill or when it meets the hot caramel, but generally can be relied upon if it is thick and cold enough.

The Fruit
It is essential that the chosen fruit is compatible with cream and sugar. Too often I have encountered *brûlées* consisting of inappropriate fruits such as apples, underripe pears and oranges. While these fruits are accessible and cheap, they are, I think, better used in other ways. No, *brûlées* only work when the fruit is right. Something a little tart that will shine through the cream and sugar is vital; for me this could be raspberries, blackberries or very lightly cooked blueberries. Something juicy such as peaches or nectarines is welcome, and the colours are appealing. To my mind, bananas are pretty much unbeatable for providing reasonably priced bulk and an affinity with thick cream.

Grapes are fine, as they enjoy being covered in caramel, and burst unexpectedly in the mouth as you eat. Redcurrants and pineapples are other tangy additions that serve a purpose. If all the fruits are sweet, that is very ripe strawberries, mango and banana, the dish will cloy. If it is to be good it needs a little bite.

The Sugar
Fine caster sugar works best for both pot-made caramel and for grilling. The unrefined variety from Billingtons works well, as do the

supermarkets' similar own brands. It is often referred to as 'golden caster sugar'. It is important that the sugar is 'clean'. In other words, there are no bits of flour or butter in there, or, heaven forbid, the lumps that appear when someone else has dipped in a wet coffee spoon.

Making the Caramel

Pot method I prefer this method for making a large *brûlée*. Put the sugar into a heavy-based deep saucepan. Thin pans are almost always pitted or warped and develop hot spots that allow the sugar to cook unevenly, burning in patches and not even melting in others. A deepish pan is essential; I once scalded myself quite badly using too shallow a pan, the hot caramel swooshing up over the edge when I grabbed it too quickly from the heat.

Incidentally, I can never get the caramel to work properly in a non-stick pan. It is also nigh impossible to see the changing colour of the caramel as it turns from shining golden caramel to throat-rasping, thick black smoke.

Pour just enough water into the pan to wet the sugar through. You can, of course, put in more, but as it has to evaporate anyway there seems little point. Put the pan over a moderate to high heat, other-wise it will take for ever. Leave the pan alone, and do not stir the mixture. If it looks as if the mixture is cooking unevenly, then move the sugar gently around the pan with a clean long-handled spoon.

When the sugar starts to turn golden, after anything from 4–15 minutes, you must keep a very close watch over it. When it becomes golden you can move the pan from side to side to encourage even colouring, but by no means stir it. When it is golden brown, but before it starts to smoke, lift it from the heat and (remembering it is blisteringly hot) pour it quickly over the cream. It will set to a crisp in parts while causing rivulets of molten cream and caramel to run down in others.

Grill method Heat the grill in advance, and get it as hot as you can. This is an overhead grill by the way. The idea is to caramelise the sugar without allowing the heat to penetrate the cream or yoghurt. Sprinkle a thin layer of absolutely clean caster sugar on top of the cream and fruit. It should be as thick as a pound coin. The cream should be as cold as you can get it. Place under the hot grill until the sugar has melted and turned golden. Unless you have a very smart grill it is likely that the sugar will caramelise unevenly, so turn the dish round to get an even tan. Invariably, this method produces a more liquid result.

The worst thing that can go wrong with either method is that a) you will burn yourself or b) you will undercook the caramel, turning it sticky, or overcook it, turning it bitter. Once *brûléed*, the dish should not be refrigerated.

Banana, Peach and Raspberry Brûlée

175g / 6oz caster sugar
700g / 1½ lb mixed bananas, peaches and raspberries
350ml / 12fl oz chilled double cream

Read the instructions on the opposite page first. Put the sugar in a heavy pan and pour in enough water to cover. Set over a medium to high flame to boil, while you prepare the fruit. Peel the bananas, stone and slice the peaches and remove any stems from the rasp-berries. Put all the fruit in a heatproof serving bowl. Although it looks wonderful in a shining cut-glass bowl, remember that it is not the easiest thing in the world to scrape encrusted caramel from a fragile glass dish.

Whip the cream until it forms stiff peaks. If it starts to look grainy then you have overwhipped it. Spoon the cream in high waves over the fruit.

The sugar in the saucepan will start to turn a pale golden caramel after 10 minutes – watch it carefully as it is prone to burning. The caramel is ready when it turns a *rich* golden brown. Immediately, taking care not to splash or burn yourself, pour the caramel over the cream and fruit. It will at once set to a crisp shiny coat. Eat within 30 minutes.

A Brûlée *of Scarlet Fruits*

175g / 6oz caster sugar
700g / 1½ lb assorted red fruits: raspberries, strawberries, redcurrants, blackberries, loganberries, etc

350g / 12oz *crème fraîche* (or double cream, whipped to soft peaks)

Follow the instructions on page 176 but do not try to whip the *crème fraîche*. Instead, spoon the cream over the fruit making peaks as best you can. Lay a few sprigs of redcurrants or little piles of berries over the peaks and then pour over the golden caramel.

Other Combinations to Try Under the Cream and Sugar

* Peaches, pineapples and mangoes

* Bananas, figs, blackberries and black grapes

* Bananas, strawberries and blueberries (the blueberries cooked briefly with a little sugar and a spoon of water till they just burst)

* Watermelons, blackberries and nectarines

* Apricots, plums and blackberries

Nectarine Yoghurt Burnt Cream

Burnt cream is just another name for a *brûlée*. Read the notes on pages 176–7 first.

You will need those sweet little white china ramekins or a shallow dish similar to a quiche plate for this. Two-thirds fill the dishes with stoned and chopped nectarines, though you could use peaches if that is what you have. Cover the fruit with thick, Greek-style yoghurt and smooth flat with the blade of a knife. Sprinkle with caster sugar, making sure you completely cover the yoghurt to the thickness of a pound coin. Place on the grill pan and cook under a preheated hot grill till the sugar starts to caramelise. Probably a couple of minutes. You may have to turn the dishes round to achieve an even effect.

* You need not stick to nectarines or even peaches. Use any ripe fruit compatible with yoghurt; try bananas, strawberries or raspberries for a start

MELONS

One of the greatest joys of shopping in France is being able to sort through the melons piled high on street market trestle tables. Picking them up and weighing them in the hand to find the heaviest for its size, and sniffing deeply to ascertain ripeness. This is heaven. I can just imagine trying to pick out the best fruit in my local street market in North London. I would probably be frogmarched down the road. And then street traders wonder why we shop at the big-name super-markets.

Melon suffered from its social position as one of three starters offered in steak bars (the others being soup of the day and prawn cocktail). The melon was invariably Honeydew, not exactly the most delectable variety, and was usually unripe. How to give a fruit a bad name.

A ripe melon, at its finest moment, is hard to improve upon. If the point of eating a fruit is its fragrance, flavour and sweet juice, then you cannot do better than a Charentais or Cantaloup melon. I can think of no other fruit which, when perfect, can give such pleasure. Unless perhaps you are picking mulberries from the tree.

Look for melons that weigh heavily and, probably, have a strong aroma, though that can be an unreliable guide as some keep their smell to themselves until cut. They should be tender, perhaps even a little soft at the stalk, though they require only a gentle squeeze to assure; prodding and poking will only damage the fruit. (I once witnessed a man in a supermarket squirt himself with a fountain of juice after being less than gentle with a Galia.)

A Somewhat Incomplete Guide to Melon Varieties

Cantaloup
This popular melon has a long season from late summer till almost Christmas. The rough, one could say scabby, greeny-yellow skin hides an orange or green flesh with a wonderful flavour. To my mind not as magnificent as the Charentais, and I think it is at its best served with slightly salty accompaniments such as Parma ham or olives.

Ogen
Ogen melons appear in midsummer and last through till late autumn. They have a green flesh beneath round yellow and green sectioned skin. Not my favourite variety, as they can sometimes be really quite watery.

Watermelon
Summer wouldn't be the same without watermelons, which are in season from July to October. Huge, dark-green cannonballs that are the very devil to get into. Rather than risk a nasty cut, it may be wiser to buy a half or quarter, which is much easier to take a slice from. The colour of the flesh varies from soft pink to bright crimson, though this is not necessarily a sign of ripeness. Flavour is not really the point here, though there can be few things I enjoy more than biting into a huge red melon slice, chilled to the point of freezing, on a roastingly hot summer's day.

Honeydew
Cheap and cheerful, sometimes a boring eat, but better than no melon at all. Recognised by its rugby-ball shape, rock-hard yellow skin and pale, watery green flesh. Its juice, though copious when ripe, is hardly the most luscious. A refreshing fruit, though, and fine for

tossing with strawberries and blackberries for a summer salad. It is pretty much available all year.

Galia

From May to September or even later, the Galia melon is always popular. Larger than an Ogen, though a relative, it is green when unripe; its netted skin turns browny yellow when ready. The flesh is often quite jelly-like and refreshing; its pale green colour and vast quantities of juice can be stirred gently into a summer fruit salad. Try adding a handful of tiny *fraises des bois*, or huge loganberries, to a bowlful of roughly chopped Galia.

Charentais

My favourite melon is the Charentais, certainly the smallest of the melons, but to my mind the finest of them all. This delectable fruit is with us from July to September only and is easily recognised by its round shape, deep segmenting and soft jade green colour. The flesh inside is a revelation, salmony-orange in colour and deeply, deeply fragrant. Cut them carefully so as not to lose any of their juices, and eat them lightly chilled. Do nothing, absolutely nothing, to a perfect specimen. Enjoy its scented flesh for what it is – possibly the finest fruit there is.

A Mélange *of Melons*

At a summer's lunch in the sunshine it would be difficult to find anything more welcome than a plate of ripe, smiling melon slices for dessert. Find your biggest plate, an oval platter, if you have one. Cover it with slices cut from as many different melons as you can lay your hands on: creamy yellow Honeydew; pale salmon-pink Charentais; green Galia; and of course, scarlet Watermelon. Arrange them in an impromptu fashion rather than following any scheme and serve them thoroughly chilled.

Melon with Raspberries and Framboise

FOR 2

1 ripe, medium melon   1 tablespoon sugar
1 tablespoon *framboise*   350g / 12oz raspberries

Cut the stalk end from the melon about 2.5cm / 1 inch or so from the top. This will form a lid. You can cut it in a zig-zag pattern if it pleases you, though I can't say it is something I would do myself. Scoop out the seeds and discard.

With a metal spoon scrape out the flesh keeping the pieces as large as possible, or you can use a melon baller if you have one. Try not to tear the melon skin, which is to act as a serving dish. Cut the melon pieces into chunks and put them into a bowl with the *framboise* and sugar. Stir gently. Spoon the melon and its juices back into the melon shell, then stir in the raspberries gently, so as not to break them up.

Chill if you can before eating. It really does look, taste and smell wonderful. Put it in the centre of the table and let each person eat it with a spoon.

Partners for Melon

Sugar and ground ginger do nothing for a melon other than insult a noble fruit. A little salt, and I do mean a little, will bring out the flavour like nothing else. So will a salty cured ham such as mountain-cured Serrano from Spain or a Parma ham from Italy. I offer the suggestion of cheese with melon to finish a meal, or for a snack in its own right. Feta, the deliciously salty white cheese from Greece, is one, as is a knob of very mature Parmesan or Pecorino. If serving a mixed plate of melon and cheese I would throw in a handful of olives too.

Tom Jaine's Melon, Redcurrants and Cassis

A recipe from Tom Jaine, former editor of *The Good Food Guide*, from his book *Cooking in the Country*, a collection of his newsletters written to regular guests at The Carved Angel restaurant in Dartmouth. I will not argue with Tom's preference for the Charentais variety, despite my earlier comments, though I might suggest that you could use another.

FOR 2

100g / 4oz caster sugar	2 punnets of redcurrants,
75ml / 3fl oz water	topped and tailed
50ml / 2fl oz Cassis	juice of ½ lemon
	1 Charentais melon

Make a syrup of the sugar and water; take off the heat, add the Cassis; add the redcurrants. Let this cool fully. Season with the lemon juice. Cut the melon into slices and scoop away the seeds. Peel the slices and cut further into thin chunks. Mix.

Honeydew and White Port

Honeydew needs a little help if it is to be good. Choose a very yellow-skinned melon and cut it roughly into large chunks, discarding the seeds. Each chunk should be large enough to fill a dessertspoon; little pieces look horrid. Sprinkle with chilled white port and chopped mint leaves. You will need three healthy-looking sprigs of mint and 3 tablespoons of white port per melon. Remember that a little mint goes a long way.

Utter Bliss

Several people lay claim to this recipe. I first came across it when working up in the English Lakes, at John Tovey's Miller Howe to be precise. This was one of the most popular dishes there, though I seem to remember it being served as a starter, which would be very much in the style of the place. This is not quite John Tovey's recipe. Believe the name.

FOR 2

a ripe, medium melon

100g / 4oz strawberries

1 tablespoon sugar

sparkling wine

Cut the melon in half. Scoop out and discard the seeds and stringy bits. Whizz the berries to a purée, sweeten with a little sugar (this is surprisingly necessary once the sparkling wine goes in). Set the melon in a serving dish so that it will not wobble. You can trim the base a little, but don't make a hole in the melon skin.

Pour some of the strawberry purée into the hollow then fill up with sparkling wine. Eat while still sparkling.

Cantaloup and Fraises des Bois

Halve the melon, scoop out the seeds losing as little of the juice as you can, then scatter over a few tiny wild strawberries. I find a tablespoon of berries just enough for half a small Cantaloup. If your fruit is a large one, then cut it into quarters or even sixths, put the slices on a generous-sized plate and throw over the little berries.

Ogen and Basil

Wonderful combination this. Tear up a handful of basil leaves or shred them with a knife, sprinkle the leaves over a small halved and seeded Ogen and eat at once while the melon is still chilled and the basil still has its pepperiness.

Melon and Honey

A good way to perk up a Honeydew or a lacklustre Ogen. Cut the fruit into large pieces, discarding the seeds, of course, and the skin.

If you have one of those dinky melon ballers you could use it to great effect here. Drop the fruit into a bowl, drizzle over about 2 tablespoons of honey per half melon and leave for 15 minutes or so before eating. Flower honeys are more suitable here than herb and heather ones, and runny honey is more successful than set.

Melon and Cheese

Not a dessert especially, but worth mentioning all the same, was a snack plate I made for myself one afternoon consisting of chunks of rather dull but juicy Honeydew melon jumbled with thin slices of sharp farmhouse Cheddar. It was really rather good, and was made in five minutes.

Melon, Peaches and Nectarines with Amaretto

Serve the three together in a salad with a sprinkling of the almond liqueur. An idea lifted from the late Jeremy Round's classic *The Independent Cook*.

Charentais and . . .

No. There is absolutely nothing that will improve a perfectly ripe, luscious Charentais. Take the soft green fruit somewhere quiet, I suggest the garden, and eat it chilled all by yourself *sans* sugar, salt, cream, berries or any other good idea that springs to mind. Any addition would be an intrusion.

Watermelon with Feta

A summer snack or original ending. Cut the watermelon into large chunks, though nothing bigger than you would put in your mouth in one go, and toss the chunks with hunks of Feta cheese, broken roughly from the block. Serve cold, with a handful of shredded basil leaves.

Melon with Blackberries

Slightly tart blackberries and ripe green-fleshed melon, Canteloup or Ogen for preference, are a delightful way to end a meal. Particularly if it has been quite rich. This combination looks its best when the melon is served in mouth-sized chunks and a few dark berries have been dotted among them in a white bowl.

CHEESES FOR SUMMER

Soft goat's cheeses, both British and French, are for many the high spot of the cheese year. Fresh goat's milk cheeses, soft, white and usually sold in fez-shaped pieces, have an unmatchable piquancy and freshness. Often sold rolled in chopped dill fronds or chives (too many to my mind), these cheeses make a charming finale to a meal. One cheese will serve two with a little bread.

A favourite pudding of mine, if you can extend the term to such an idea, is to put a smooth white goat's cheese in the centre of a smooth white plate and scatter round whole strawberries, their leaves intact to hold on to. As I eat, I spread each berry with a generous mouthful of cheese.

British cheesemakers are currently producing some of the best goat's cheeses around. Names to look out for are: Golden Cross, a dense, tart, ash-covered log made in Sussex; Innes, charming little cheeses sometimes flavoured with rosemary or oregano; Perroche, made in Kent and has a clean, fresh flavour.

Of the cow's milk varieties, Pont l'Evêque, from Normandy, is very much a summer cheese. A good one will be like a plump, square cushion, an amber to soft pumpkin in colour with sweet, tangy flesh. What I call a knife and fork cheese, best eaten without any accompaniment, even bread.

Other summer cheeses include sweet, earthy, semi-soft mountain Reblochon, salty, tangy, crumbly Feta (even the plastic-wrapped stuff is okay, especially when eaten in alternate mouthfuls with fresh raw peas), and white, crumbly Ricotta, the Italian fresh cheese. Make sure that the Ricotta is brilliant white, crumbly and moist. Don't buy any that is yellowing, it taints easily, and loses its subtle freshness quicker than most. Equally good, though as different a mouthful as you can get, is a mature Parmesan. A tangy, deeply savoury bite, just break off a lump with a short sharp knife and munch it as you clear away the supper things.

Acknowledgements

Recipes must come from somewhere. They don't just hit you like a bolt from the blue when you are doing the ironing or feeding the cat. For the most part I have acknowledged my sources and inspirations in the text, but there will be omissions. I would like to thank the authors and cooks who have given me permission to use their recipes and quotes and, in particular, those whose good ideas I have mercilessly exploited to my own ends. I am grateful, too, to Fay Maschler for letting me quote from her column in the *Evening Standard*, to Sophie Grigson for allowing me to use her words from the *Independent*, and to Lynda Brown for her advice and inspiration.

Once again my thanks to Louise Haines, my editor at Michael Joseph, for her patience and for turning a chaotic manuscript into a readable book. My thanks, too, to Christabel Gairdner, and to Nancy Roberts, my editor at *marie claire*, for her patience and continuing support.

Bibliography

Battiscombe, Georgina, *English Picnics*, Harvill Press, 1949

Beard, James, *American Cookery*, Hart-Davies, 1975

Bissell, Frances, *The Pleasures of Cooking*, Chatto & Windus, 1986

Bissell, Frances, *Sainsbury's Book of Food*, 1989

Brown, Catherine, *Scottish Cookery*, Richard Drew, 1985

Brown, Lynda, *The Cook's Garden*, Century, 1990

Bunyard, Edward, *The Anatomy of Dessert*, Chatto & Windus, 1933

Child, Julia, *The Way to Cook*, Alfred Knopf, 1989

Christian, Glynn, *Glynn Christian's Delicatessen Handbook*, Macdonald, 1982

Costa, Margaret, *The Four Seasons Cookery Book*, Nelson, 1970

Crabtree and Evelyn Cookbook, Barrie and Jenkins, 1989

Croft-Cooke, Rupert, *English Cooking*, W. H. Allen, 1960

David, Elizabeth, *A Book of Mediterranean Food*, John Lehmann, 1950

David, Elizabeth, *French Provincial Cooking*, Michael Joseph, 1960

David, Elizabeth, *Summer Cooking*, Museum Press, 1955

Davidson, Alan and Knox, Charlotte, *Fruit*, Mitchell Beazley, 1991

Del Conte, Anna, *Entertaining All'Italiana*, Bantam, 1991

Gavin, Paola, *Italian Vegetarian Cookery*, Optima, 1991

Graham, Peter, *Classic Cheese Cookery*, Penguin, 1988

Gray, Patience, *Honey from a Weed*, Prospect Books, 1986

Grigson, Jane, *Good Things*, Michael Joseph, 1971

Grigson, Jane, *Jane Grigson's Fruit Book*, Michael Joseph, 1982

Grigson, Sophie, *Sophie Grigson's Ingredients Book*, Pyramid, 1991

Hambro, Natalie, *Particular Delights*, Norman and Hobhouse, 1981

Hazan, Marcella, *Classic Italian Cookbook*, Macmillan, 1980

Heath, Ambrose, *Good Savouries*, Faber & Faber, 1939

Hegarty, Patricia, *An English Flavour*, Equation, 1988

Holt, Geraldene, *Geraldene Holt's Complete Book of Herbs*, Conran Octopus, 1991

Jaine, Tom, *Cooking in the Country*, Chatto & Windus, 1986

Lassalle, George, *East of Orphanides*, Kyle Cathie, 1991

Madison, Deborah, *Greens Cookbook*, Bantam, 1988

Maschler, Fay, *Eating In*, Bloomsbury, 1987

Molyneaux, Joyce, *The Carved Angel Cookery Book*, Collins, 1990

Nicholson, B. E., *Oxford Book of Food Plants*, Oxford University Press, 1969

Pomaine, Edouard de, *Cooking In Ten Minutes*, Cookery Book Club, 1969

Rance, Patrick, *The Great British Cheese Book*, Macmillan, 1983

Roden, Claudia, *A New Book of Middle Eastern Food*, Viking, 1985

Round, Jeremy, *The Independent Cook*, Barrie and Jenkins, 1985

Shere, Lindsey R., *Chez Panisse Desserts*, Random House, 1985

Slater, Nigel, *Real Fast Food*, Michael Joseph, 1992

Slater, Nigel, *The Marie Claire Cook Book*, Paul Hamlyn, 1992

Smith, Delia, *Delia Smith's Complete Cookery Course*, BBC Books, 1978

Smith, Michael, *Afternoon Tea*, Macmillan, 1986

Stobart, Tom, *Spices, Herbs and Flavourings*, Penguin, 1987

Toklas, Alice B., *The Alice B. Toklas Cookbook*, Michael Joseph, 1954

Waters, Alice, *Chez Panisse Menu Cookbook*, Chatto & Windus, 1982

Whiteaker, Stafford, *The Compleat Strawberry*, Crown, 1985

Index